SOMETIMES
A GREAT NATION

Sometimes a Great Nation, A Photo
Album of Canada, 1850-1925 ©1984 by
Edward Cavell and Altitude Publishing
Ltd., Box 490, Banff, Alberta, Canada
T0L 0C0
All Rights Reserved
ISBN 0-919381-13-8

Cavell, Edward, 1948 –
    Sometimes a great nation

ISBN 0-919381-13-8

1. Canada – History – Pictorial works.
I. Title.
FC174.C38 1984   971'.0022'2   C84-091349-4
F1026.C38 1984

SOMETIMES
A GREAT NATION

A Photo Album *of* Canada

—— 1850 ~ 1925 ——

🌿

Edward Cavell

𝐴

Altitude Publishing Ltd.

For my friends. In appreciation of your inspiration, support, patience, and gentle criticism.

CONTENTS

William Armstrong (left) and Willian Napier, photographed in Toronto,
wearing fancy-dress buckskins. As surveyors and artists in the period before
photography these men were responsible for creating the visual record of a
new land. Napier was with the Red River Exploring Expedition in 1857, the
first western reconnaissance to be sponsored by a Canadian government.
Always the artist and draughtsman, Armstrong worked on several rail lines in
central Canada and was chief engineer on the expedition sent to quell the
Red River Rebellion in 1870. He was also a principal in Armstrong, Beere &
Hime, engineers and photographers, one of the earliest photographic firms in
Canada. Humphrey Lloyd Hime, assigned to the Assiniboine and
Saskatchewan Expedition in 1858, was the first to photograph the western
plains of British North America. This hand-coloured salt print, dated 1858,
was probably made by one of the partners in that firm.

INTRODUCTION

T HIS IS NOT A HISTORY. It's a visual journal, a personal account of a journey of discovery. It's the chronicle of a voyage into the past. It's a romance, the record of a courtship of a country. It's a surprise, a fantasy, an adventure, a realization of who we are. It's a photo album of the Canadian family during a seventy-five-year period in which both our nation and self image were formed. It's a personal, eclectic, often whimsical selection of photographs that skip like rounded stones across the vast pool of our visual heritage.

Canada and photography entered the new world of the industrial age arm in arm, new entities in a society being propelled into the future by the power of steam. A new nation, the child of an expanding world, Canada matured through a period of social revolution unequalled at any time. Science and technology expanded the boundaries of the Victorian world beyond any previous conception. An integral part and logical extension of the technological society, photography recorded both the birth and maturing of the new nation and was a profound influence on the lives of its inhabitants. The legacy of the photographic image allows us to view ourselves in context with what has gone before. The hue and patina of the vintage prints confirm an almost physical bond with our past. Like a cabinet of curiosities, photographs yield a plethora of details and subtle realizations. The minutiae allow us to conceive a more complete vision of the whole.

This book is based on the belief that photographs, compelling and beautiful visual objects in themselves, are a fascinating reflection of ourselves and our past. A multitude of images, covering seventy-five years in the history of a nation, has been condensed into a selection of fewer than two hundred photographs. A subjective exercise, the selection is occasionally logical (the image illuminated a historical theme dear to my heart); quite often it's emotional (the photograph touched an aspect of my soul and demanded to be seen). The whimsical and the sensational have had a definite influence. Finally, there is a desire to share an appreciation of the aesthetics of a well-made photograph and the unique beauty of vintage photographic processes. Winnowed from the millions of photographs held in archives across Canada, these images represent a very personal discovery of our country.

🌺　　🌺　　🌺

GROWING UP CANADIAN IS A BEWILDERING EXERCISE in cultural masochism. Immersed in a cynical folklore from birth, we perpetuate the negative mythology that has become the most obvious aspect of our national character. In the face of the reality of a stunningly beautiful, progressive country with one of the world's highest living standards, we continue the running gag that places our national ego somewhere between those of Greenland and Lesotho. As pragmatists and stalwart individualists we reject national heroes as vainglorious. In this ultimate democracy, the equality of all Canadians prevents any from rising in the estimation of the others. We persist in diminishing ourselves. In the Canadian experience, the victors who might become national heroes stand as constant reminders of the possibility of civil war. The victory cry turns to dust in the mouth, to be chewed into a compromise and swallowed down like medicine so that victor and vanquished may survive together. To this day, Canadians are haunted by their vanquished peoples – the French Canadians, the Métis, the Indians and the Inuit. The ways of the native people continue to fascinate us. The donning of Indian costume remains a photo event, if only for our political leaders; and the Eskimo parka has become standard winter gear across the land.

If victors we ever had, they are now the guilt-ridden WASPs, and our most celebrated rebel, Louis Riel, whose Métis-Indian insurrections spurred the imposition of Canadian Dominion in the west, has been established as a hero on the lawn of the Manitoba Legislature. In a way, we are a nation of losers, joined, through immigration, by the victims and vanquished of almost every other country in the world. Irish immigration brought an active civil war to Canada, and to the United States, where Irish republic-ans, known as Fenians, continued their fight against Britain by launching raids into Canada. It was a Fenian who assassinated one of the Fathers of Confederation, D'Arcy McGee, an Irish immigrant himself, who, in 1862, enunciated the only possible doctrine of Canadian nationality: "A Canadian nationality, not French-Canadian, nor British-Canadian, nor Irish-Canadian – patriotism rejects the prefix – is, in my opinion, what we should look forward to, that is what we ought to labour for, that is what we ought to be prepared to defend to the death…[we should] cultivate that true catholicity of spirit which embraces all creeds, all classes, and all races, in order to make our boundless province, so rich in known and unknown resources, a great new northern nation."

🍁　🍁　🍁

IF OUR IMPERFECT MULTI-CULTURALISM HAS FAILED to produce a self realization of greatness, it has allowed our national survival. We may celebrate the Gothic perfection of the Parliamentary Library at Ottawa, the neo-classic glories of the Manitoba Legislature, the pastoral charm of a Quebec village, and the spectacular beauty of Niagara Falls and the Rockies. It is the railway, with its clangorous, leviathan equipment and monumental bridges and trestles, that provides the images of the only victory that we may all embrace – victory over the overwhelming geography that still dwarfs us. Canadians have earned their greatness in transportation and communication, in building the basic networks that bind together every conceivable kind of terrain, in all extremes of temperate and Arctic climates. We have earned our greatness by pushing the wheat frontier beyond the limits of northern climate, by growing vegetable marrows in Edmonton, by developing world-champion milk cows, by digging some of the deepest mines in the world, by building Lunenburg dories and the fastest ships under sail.

This book presents images of Canada from roughly 1850 to 1925. Seventy-five years is hardly a hiccough in geological time but it is a long life in human terms. It's a very short period for an entity as complex as a nation to develop a sense of itself, especially the Gordian knot that is Canada. The colonial tradition imposes a lower estimation of the colony in view of the homeland, the population gaining strength and identity through the power of the British Empire. The Empire has gone, but Canadians still maintain a loyalty to the British Crown, an allegiance that is the basis of our parliamentary form of government. In this way, Canadians still cling to colonialism, unable to isolate a colonial period as cherished history, forever (it seems) arguing about national identity. Even so, the images in this book bear witness to the development of a unique nation and present the quintessential Canadian acknowledgement that we are sometimes a great nation.

🌿   🌿   🌿

IN THE MID-NINETEENTH CENTURY THERE WERE SEVEN BRITISH COLONIES in the northern half of North America: Newfoundland, Nova Scotia, New Brunswick, Prince Edward Island, the Province of Canada (the union of Upper and Lower Canada), British Columbia and Vancouver Island. Unique unto themselves, they answered only to Britain. Sharing the continent with a former enemy, these bites of British imperialism were notched into a huge landscape that was wilderness beyond comprehension. Roads were few and local, communication was by sea, and mainly under sail. Like most other people in the world, the colonials were interested mainly in their own survival, property and community. News of world events was slow in spreading and affected them only slightly – except in matters of trade. The British North American colonies were isolated from each other by the wilderness that was their only resource. As part of the Empire, they considered themselves a civilized lid on what was perceived to be a boiling, anarchistic republic to the south.

The United States in the nineteenth century was the bully on the block. Rich, progressive, adventurous, from day one the country had a glow on. The siren song of the sunny south was at once a sweet temptation and anathema to the British colonials. They were brothers in our endeavours – cultural siblings, fellow pioneers on a virgin continent, strangers in a new land, taming a vast and awe-inspiring wilderness. But we were the Empire and they were the rebels, separated by different traditions of law, identity and affiliation.

The American doctrine of Manifest Destiny was an ever-present threat to the British colonies. In the period between 1845 and 1898 the United States annexed Texas, New Mexico, Arizona, Nevada, California, Oregon, Washington, and Hawaii. The Americans had purchased Alaska from the Russians and invaded Puerto Rico, Cuba, Guam, and the Philippines. We were surrounded and definitely outnumbered. Unwittingly the Americans became the one necessary common foe that forged the emotional bond that would unite the separate and scattered colonies into a nation.

Britain's opting for free trade in 1849 was an enforced weaning for the British colonies around the world. Bursting with the benefits of industrialization, the mother country was finding that the system of protective tariffs that bound the colonies to her was becoming a major hindrance. Beyond that, the more settled (white) colonies were becoming a nuisance. The marginal returns were outweighed by their conflicting demands of autonomy and assistance. Compared to more exotic parts of the Empire, Canada was especially bothersome and uninteresting. The cold colony was indefensible and a probable source of conflict with the United States, which was a major area for investment and an important trade partner.

Rather than being disaffected because they were abandoned, the colonies reacted by being more fervent about the concept of the Empire. They were anxious to maintain contact with the homeland and desperate to retain an identity with more substance than a poor colony could supply. The expression of loyalty to the Crown occasioned by the parade of royal visits was the only possible patriotism. Images of the visits highlighted the lives of several Canadian generations, allowing them a brief moment in the pomp and panoply of the Empire. The soaring archway erected in Halifax to symbolize the vaulting imperial power for the 1860 visit by the Prince of Wales was adapted at other sites to celebrate everything from cheese to economic policies.

🌿   🌿   🌿

THE ROMANTIC CONCEPT OF THE EMPIRE created a rare bond between English and French populations during the early nineteenth century. The notion of being a part of the greatest civilizing force of all time was very attractive. The Empire was viewed as a divine light in a dark world, a manifestation of the British sense of Christian duty to the lesser races. If, while straining under the "white man's burden", an individual could improve his station in society and amass a modest wealth, wasn't that simply a just reward for bringing civilization to the heathen savage? French Canadians could easily agree with the Christian and intellectual goals of the Empire. It was more difficult, however, to accept the imperialist stance.

The new technology of the railroads meant that the weak emotional bond of Empire could be reinforced with steel in British North America. Individuals with vision realized that if the central colonies (Canada) could be bound to New Brunswick and Nova Scotia by rail, a railroad could bind the entire northern half of the continent to the Empire. The vision of an all-British land and sea route to the Orient was magic and irresistible. It was also quite impossible. The territory that had to be crossed was terra incognita, a virtually blank map with unknown dragons.

The expanded awareness and shrinking world created by the steam engine, a basic fear of expropriation by the United States and the general fervour of the furtherance of the Empire resulted in the confederation of the British North American colonies in 1867. It was a pragmatic act to create an illogical nation that was economically unsound, geographically impossible and culturally divided. Rather than being created out of a generally accepted philosophical belief shared by the population, Canada was created for lack of a better idea. The visionary few managed to convince a portion of the population that there was no alternative, in particular, no alternative to the American presence. In the words of D'Arcy McGee: "I do not believe it is our destiny to be engulfed into a Republican union ... it seems to me that we have theatre enough under our feet to act another and a worthier part; we can hardly join the Americans on our own terms, and we never ought to join them on theirs."

The contractual requirement of a rail link to bring British Columbia into Confederation (not to mention the necessity of transporting troops, learned during Riel's Red River Rebellion in 1870) turned steel into the stuff of a new imperial dream: a *Canadian* Empire from ocean to ocean.

Under the guidance of Sir John A. Macdonald and the other Fathers of Confederation the territorial dream was to grow to immense proportions. In 1870 Manitoba became a tiny province. That same year the Hudson's Bay Company's territories were added, comprising a tract of land that included the balance of Western Canada, the North West Territories, Northern Ontario and Northern Quebec. In 1871 British Columbia joined. (It had merged with Vancouver Island in 1866.) In 1873 Prince Edward Island finally succumbed and the Arctic islands claimed by Britain were ceded to Canada in 1880. Only Newfoundland remained apart. A nation was created that was forty times the size of the mother country.

The new nation was greeted by most of the new Canadians with all the enthusiasm of a sulking child being dragged off to visit a least favourite relative. Even the name Canada (probably an adaptation of the Iroquois word Kanata meaning a cabin or a lodge) was a compromise, settled on after a consideration of heart-stirring alternatives like Tuponia (standing for The United Provinces of North America), Hochelaga (the Indian village where Montreal now stands), Cabotia, Borealia, Transatlantica and Efisga – an acronym for English, French, Irish, Scottish, German, and the Aboriginal Islands. Considering the alternatives the residents of the new nation were still not overjoyed by the name selected.

The inhabitants of Canada may have accepted the idea of the new nation rather grudgingly but in the tradition of pioneer-immigrant nations, the overall atmosphere was positive and there were faint stirrings of national pride. The country was growing rapidly and generally prospering although it would rise and fall in the estimation of its inhabitants in direct relation to the health of their pocketbooks. Threats of separation would arise from Nova Scotia to British Columbia as the disgruntled population battled with the domineering self-righteous central provinces. Failing a better idea, we would remain Canadian. The perpetual tone and substance of Canadian political rhetoric was determined very early.

Canada was a child of the empire, internally autonomous yet dependent on Great Britain for all aspects of external affairs. Unfortunately, the inevitable British policy in exercising the imperial prerogative in territorial disputes with the United States was to placate the bristling Americans, both to avoid an unwinnable war and protect her extensive investments. Virtually every claim on Britain's territory in North America was decided in favour of the obstreperous Americans. Canadians were forced into a difficult, love-hate relationship with the mother country.

Compared to the blood and glories of the rest of the Empire – exotic India, the orient trade, tropical climates – Canada's placid agrarian population and legendary winters generated little romance. A few aberrant Brits may have fancied a life in the snowy wild amongst the noble savages or ventured into wheat farming and fruit ranching, or indulged as tourists in the thrill of the hunt. Canada had become the domain of the pragmatic immigrant looking for land and a new, prosperous, and stable life.

Canada's reputation as a cold, frumpy, poor cousin was a mixture of reality and a holdover from the fur trade days when it was advantageous to maintain a low profile. This dowdy appearance protected the new nation from any further manifestations of American Manifest Destiny. With the exception of the

Alaskan Boundary dispute in 1903 the Americans had won the last of their many and various claims on British territory in 1872, when Kaiser Wilhelm I of Germany, acting as arbitrator, awarded them the San Juan Islands between Vancouver Island and the mainland. This followed the treaty of 1846 when the myopic British government relinquished the Oregon Territory. (It was the common rumour of the day that the British negotiators gave the Pacific Northwest away because they had been informed that the salmon fishing on the Columbia River wasn't particularly good.)

There was little left of apparent worth. The American belief that the remaining British holdings would just naturally be assimilated took the edge off any aggressive stance. The American Secretary of State, W.H. Seward, declared in 1867, "I know that Nature designs that this whole continent, not just these thirty-six states, shall be, sooner or later, within the magic circle of the American Union." This slight oversight saved Canada until after the First World War, when the shift in world politics made tampering with the world's longest undefended border an embarrassment for the United States.

Britain didn't take the sabre-rattling too seriously. All of the British regular troops in Canada, except for a small contingent in Halifax, were withdrawn in 1871. The tiny, ill-trained, Canadian Militia was left very much alone. Macdonald reacted to the problem by suggesting that in the event of American aggression the Indian Army invade San Francisco and hold it hostage in return for the safety of Montreal and Toronto.

The Royal Engineers were sent out to finish marking the boundary along the 49th Parallel. The work had been started on the Pacific coast in 1858 in reaction to the gold rush that was bringing hordes of American miners to British Columbia. The outbreak of the American Civil War halted the marking process at the American Great Divide in the Rocky Mountains in 1862. In 1872-74 the vast open prairie between Lake of the Woods and the mountains was dotted every few miles with a sod mound supporting an iron post, marking a conceptual wall that supplied safe haven to the north for Sitting Bull and his Sioux after the Little Big Horn, and freedom in the south for Louis Riel after the Red River Rebellion.

The new nation grew much more slowly than anticipated. The completion of the Canadian Pacific Railway in 1885 did not result in the expected flood of immigration but rather a trickle. The cornucopia to the south drew off most prospective immigrants as well as a significant number of young English and French Canadians. The American dream (and active promotion of fertile land) was too hard to resist. By the turn of the century most of the good land available in the United States had been taken up and a reverse immigration occurred into the Canadian West. With less distraction from the United States, European immigration reached the levels that had been expected twenty years earlier. The West filled up rapidly, causing an unprecedented building boom. Sir Wilfrid Laurier's statement that "the twentieth century belongs to Canada" summed up the overwhelming optimism that pervaded the land.

The complexion of the Canadian population was changed forever by the cultural diversity of the new immigrants. Increasingly fewer people had any connection with the United Kingdom. Along with the eastern European immigrants the English-speaking population was becoming increasingly American or native born. Second and third generations of Canadians were finding themselves in the perplexing situation of professing loyalty to a royal personage in a land they had never seen.

The French Canadians were in the only land they had known for three centuries; any bonds with Europe were weak and conceptual at best. A population of slightly over two million by 1911 had basically grown from fewer than ten thousand original seventeenth- and eighteenth-century immigrants. They drew their strength and inspiration from the church and the land to which they had been bound for generations.

New immigrants to the sparsely populated West did not encounter a strong indigenous culture. Apart from the necessity to learn the English language, there was little pressure to subordinate their own rich cultures in communities largely composed of their countrymen. One of the strongest cultural influences in the Canadian West was the myth of the American Wild West. The new settlers joyfully indulged in the ever-popular pastime of dressing up and play acting at being cowboy desperadoes.

🍁 🍁 🍁

THE TWENTIETH CENTURY WAS INITIATED BY WAR. Seven thousand Canadians fought for the Empire in the Boer War (1899-1902). By 1918 sixty thousand Canadians had died for the Empire in the War to End All Wars. The First World War was a pivotal point in the history of the modern world. Old nations disappeared, new ones formed. Canadians had for the first time fought and died as Canadians in a distinct (and respected) unit in the Allied forces. This fact has caused most historians to regard the Canadian war effort as the birthpangs of the Canadian identity. The scale of the slaughter had to mean something! The level of carnage on the part of all nations did result in the well-intentioned if ineffective League of Nations. Canada's exceptional loss was recognized by the other founding nations, which allowed the young country to join independently from Britain; it was the first international recognition of Canada as a sovereign state.

Historically, war has been the traditional measure of the progress of nations. The chronology of great feats of valour, cities laid waste, battles won and lost, the body count, become the lexicon of national identity. The devastation of the First World War meant that Canada had finally earned its place in the ranks of ancient nations. The sense of sadness and loss developed into pride, and meaning was ascribed to something that made no sense. The war did little to create a Canadian national identity; if anything, the aspects of division and conflict were reinforced English Canadians fought and died to save the mother country, colonial sons coming to the defense of the Empire. Many French Canadians refused to partici- pate in what they considered a foreign, imperialist war. The contribution made by those who did go to war was hidden from view by the violent reaction against enforced conscription. English Canadians were embittered and had little understanding of the French reticence.

Friction between English and French has been an ever-present aspect of Canadian life, the ebb and flow of racial passions guiding our political realities. The relatively positive period of cautious respect that had developed between French and English in the period that followed the British conquest was soon destroyed by Old World bigotries imported on the tide of immigration caused by the Irish potato famine of 1846. The powerful Protestant Orange Order (named for William of Orange) arrived in Canada and the Orangemen soon focused their hatred for all Catholics on the French. Victorian society was a rigid world of right and wrong, black and white. There was little appreciation of cultural differences. No quarter was given as the true faith was preached from the pulpits of Christian Canada: in Roman Catholic churches the imperialist English were doomed to hell; in the Protestant churches the French papists were declared instruments of the devil. Historian Arthur Lower describes Canada at this time as "more British than the Queen, more Catholic than the Pope." In light of the history of the Anti-Chinese Societies in British Columbia, the Ku Klux Klan all across the West, and the Orange Lodges in Ontario, it's a mystery where the myth of Canadian racial tolerance developed.

🌱   🌱   🌱

THE WANING EMPIRE AFTER THE WAR meant an increased international image for Canada. The imperial connection began to break down. With the enactment of the Statute of Westminster in 1931, Canada was in effect granted final independence and made an equal of Great Britain; only a few legal and technical political connections were maintained. The image of being a servant of the Empire would take a long time to dispel, however. There was no such thing as a Canadian citizen until January 1, 1947. Canadians travelled outside Canada as British subjects until 1971. Before 1931 Canadian domestic law was subject to review by the British Parliament and legal issues could be appealed to the Imperial Privy Council.

Aspects of national identity had been growing slowly over the years but English Canada was caught unprepared for the severing of the imperial bonds. We were cut adrift in the world with nothing to replace the glories of Empire but the self-depreciating colonial image of the boring, provincial, woodsy Canadian that had been cynically fostered since the first French settlements. Any faint stirrings of national pride were buried under feelings of being deserted in a cultural backwater. The fear that under the plaid jacket and wool tuque there was nothing but a vacuum, faintly echoing the refrain from *Rose Marie*, prevented most Canadians from even attempting to consider a national identity. For lack of an alternative we continued the tradition of colonial self-effacement, taking perverse delight in negative lore. We take joy in the belief that the name Canada comes from the Spanish *Aca nada*, which means "nothing there." We revel in Voltaire's assessment of Canada as "just a few acres of snow."

The multiplicity of cultures in Canada and the extreme geographical variations have generated a very complex history and have made it virtually impossible for a unifying concept to evolve. There is no single consistent thread to Canadian history, no linear thought or concept that can be used as a focus. Every statement must be qualified, every fact multiplied by the number of regions or races affected. If ever there is accord between the English and French of central Canada then there is the certainty that the Maritimes or the West are disaffected. The ever-present exception to the rule makes it impossible to conceive of Canada in any categorical sense. Rather than developing a positive view of who or what we are, we have defined ourselves by default, in a land described by poet Patrick Anderson as "a chance, a dance that is not danced." Not being American, or British, or European, we are Canadian, our identity not a character but a sense of difference.

❧ ❧ ❧

A NATIONAL IDENTITY IS AS VISUAL AS IT IS IDEOLOGICAL. How we perceive ourselves is how we are perceived by others and – in a self-perpetuating loop – how we perceive ourselves. It's all too easy to be totally preoccupied with non-Hollywood imperfections, rather than concentrate on our natural strengths. Our image of the present is an extension of the past, built piecemeal from millions of visual elements. Each image becomes an essential link in a visual genetic code. Unspoken, quietly pervasive, our visual identity, like red hair, is passed on through generations. Certain images have ingrained themselves in our Canadian collective consciousness; the Last Spike, a Mountie embracing some sweet young thing, a Krieghoff snowshoer, or perhaps a Tom Thomson sky.

From the time of cave dwellers, the visual history of the world has been recorded by artists and artisans. The image of reality has been rendered in stylized and often quite abstracted forms by the human hand; Egyptians walk sideways, Romans decapitate. European painters discovered the technique of perspective during the Renaissance; images of the world were more realistic but the content was filtered through the expectations and stylized norms of society. Fallen heroes like Wolfe at Quebec were illustrated as characters in a European melodrama.

Paintings of the New World created in the eighteenth and early nineteenth centuries were bound to the European tradition. The North American wilderness and its inhabitants were rendered in a way to conform to the sensibilities of the more cultural, alien, European world. Romantic images of a wilderness turned into the English countryside were accepted by a colonial population anxious to adopt an air of culture. Exaggeration was normal and accepted, everything was made more picturesque; the mountains were higher, the country was prettier, the natives were more savage or more noble.

The Victorian world was fascinated with detail. Everything was being investigated, enumerated and catalogued. It was the time of Louis Agassiz, who expanded the world of the natural sciences into a credible field of study. Art critic John Ruskin convinced an entire civilization of the beauties of the wilderness, from the minute to the sublime. In 1858, the year that the first photograph was taken of the Canadian prairies, Charles Darwin made public his theories on evolution. The medium of photography was the logical response of the scientific age: the master of detail, the medium dedicated to minutiae.

❧ ❧ ❧

BASED ON OPTICAL THEORIES KNOWN FOR CENTURIES and the observation that sunlight affected silver salts, photography arrived in the 1830s, "invented" by several individuals working separately. At first an oddity, a static reality captured in minute detail on a silvered plate, the magic art was soon to pervade all aspects of modern life. Not just a reflection of a cultural revolution, photography was also a major influence in social change. Photographs of the new western lands promoted immigration (some hopefuls attracted to the East Kootenays in British Columbia were surprised to find that the bounteous fruit shown in the pictures had been wired to the trees). John Joseph Kelso, a Toronto social reformer and humanitarian, used photography extensively to illustrate the suffering of children; he founded the Toronto Humane Society and the Children's Aid Society. Toronto photographer Arthur Goss documented both the squalor of slum conditions and the energetic urban renewal and public health programs that were introduced after the turn of the century.

Photography became an essential record of everyday life. Professional or amateur photographers became commonplace at all occasions from major historical events to the minor triumphs of ordinary folk. Before photography, history had been the private preserve of the privileged. He who generated the most paper (and preserved it) would be sure to be remembered; politicians, academics and tycoons were guaranteed a place in history. Through photography, the achievements of any individual could be documented and left as a record of the continuity of society. The photograph was proof-positive of one's existence and a legacy for one's family. A record of sporting events, store fronts, home and children – things that would have merited only passing mention in any written account – now existed in irrefutable detail. Photographs became a reflection of an individual's pride and accomplishments, an illustration to the folks back home that life in the colony – or on the frontier – was indeed milk and honey. During the earlier days of photography, the process had the importance of the unique. It was possible for the photographer to get the entire population of a small town to change into their best clothes to be photographed. The basic act of taking a photograph made the event or place something of note and worth the effort of posing.

Photographs were and are a talisman of personal memories and a source of dreams, exotic visions of distant lands or an intimate connection with a loved one no longer present. The ultimate democratic art form, photography was the great equalizer. The faces of the famous became as easily recognized as a next-door neighbour. Kings and Queens graced the pages of the family photo album, sharing space with Aunt Tillie and Uncle Fred. Through prints and the printed page, the images and events of the world, both benign and malignant, were exposed to the masses. Death and celebration became intimates of people who had been previously protected by the limitations of the written word.

Stereo photography (based on the phenomenon of binocular vision, in which the mind fuses two images into one three-dimensional picture) became a fad in the 1860s and continued until the First World War. Virtually every parlour had a hand viewer and sets of stereo photographs from around the world, the equivalent entertainment of today's television.

Visual information now had a veracity that had previously been impossible. The photograph was imbued with the myth of reality – the camera couldn't lie. Before the advent of direct reproduction techniques (the halftone process, still used in newspapers and magazines today, was introduced in the late 1880s), the illustrated newspapers printed "from a photograph" under the wood-block prints that filled their pages – absolute proof of the accuracy of the image. The unquestionable accuracy of the photograph spawned a new form of visual humour in the form of exaggerated paste-up composites – a wagon carrying fish the size of whales or wheat standing as tall as sugarcane. Photographing the impossible became a bit of a mania. Wisps of smoke and partly exposed figures became ghosts. Hannah Maynard, a photographer and spiritualist living in Victoria, produced extraordinary multiple-exposure tableaus in her studio that brought her departed back to life and placed the living in the other world. Many photographers used the composite technique to create magical renderings of massive group events, posing each individual separately in the studio and pasting the result into the group mounted on a painted background.

Initially photography was limited, the equipment bulky and the techniques time consuming. The earliest popular photographic processes were like modern Polaroid prints – one-shot single images. These beautiful and very delicate daguerreotypes and ambrotypes had to be treated as precious objects and were presented under glass, with brass matts, in special cases. The need for a system that could generate numerous prints of the same image eventually led to the invention of the collodion process in 1851. The negative-to-positive print system, which is still basically used today, had begun. George Eastman's mass-market Kodak, introduced in 1888, ensured that virtually all aspects of life would be under the scrutiny of the camera.

The technical limitations of the medium added additional character to the record produced. The awkwardness of the tripodal camera and the lack of sensitivity of the emulsions required long exposures that resulted in rather stiff, overly composed, static views. People rarely looked as severe and uncomfortable as portrayed. They weren't photographed because they looked that way, they looked that way because they were being photographed. The very real difficulties of overcoming the low light levels indoors ensured that most photographs were made outside.

Advances in techniques over the years allowed an increasing degree of spontaneity for both the photographer and the subject. The nature of the negative defines the capacity of the photograph to capture a scene; the sensitivity of the emulsion to light determines the amount of action possible. At mid-century, exposures were slow, requiring the subject to be absolutely still for ten seconds to several minutes. By the turn of the century exposures were measured in fractions of a second; the stiff, posed look of the 1860s became the gay nineties. Emulsions, which at first were produced on the spot (wet collodion) and required a barely portable darkroom, later became pre-packaged gelatine dry plates, requiring only a light-tight plate holder. The introduction of flexible film bases in the late 1880s resulted in much smaller and more portable cameras that allowed the photographers to respond quickly to a scene or event.

The various types of photographic printing papers also affected the nature of the picture. Early processes were very slow; the print was made, by sunlight, in contact with the negative. If a large print were desired, a large negative (occasionally as big as twenty-two by twenty-eight inches) was necessary, and therefore a mammoth camera. The advent of more sensitive enlarging papers allowed production of the smaller roll film camera.

The earliest and most basic salt prints of the 1850s were slightly rough in texture and warm in tone. Albumen prints, which remained the standard process until the 1880s, provided impeccable detail and hues ranging from purple to sepia to bitter chocolate, depending on treatment and aging. Gelatine emulsion papers introduced at the end of the nineteenth century are still with us today, and range in tone from the albumen hues to the neutral black and white that is our familiar snapshot fare.

A plethora of photographic processes appeared in the first hundred years of photography. Many were short-lived; some have survived to today. The bright blue of cyanotype, which uses iron salts instead of silver, still appears in modern blueprints; the glorious, subtle, warm grey tones of the platinum print disappeared from common use as the metal became increasingly rare and expensive. The bulky glass lantern slides, often coloured by hand, were replaced by the modern 35-mm transparency.

In retrospect, we have to consider the failings as well as the strengths of photography. In our modern world, subjected to the constant bombardment of photographic images, we have developed a casual, indifferent attitude towards photographs. We have learned that photos do lie – from the glitzy, sparkling ad man's product to the biased photos of some photo-journalists or government agencies. With the exception of pictures of a photographer's feet or the inside of camera bags, the camera doesn't take pictures by itself. There is a thinking, responding and biased (negative or positive, depending on our own position) mind guiding the omnipotent lens.

In the nineteenth and early twentieth centuries photography was principally a tool, a means of recording something for fun or profit. With a few notable exceptions the bulk of photographs were overwhelmingly dull, produced on demand to capture some long forgotten significance in the daily march of life. The vast majority are assembly-line portraits of non-dynamic people and pictures of every group of more than two in uniforms or funny hats. They were made to record an event, for reasons as simple as a ball game, as arcane as a Masonic Lodge. By sheer weight of numbers they are impressive. People had an intense desire to be photographed, to be immortalized.

In order to better understand the nature of the visual record left to us, there are several aspects we must understand. During the Victorian period, photography, apart from the ever-present inexpensive portrait, was the exclusive property of the middle and upper classes – those who could afford the time and expense to indulge in photography as a hobby or pay the fees of a professional photographer. The poor and the oppressed, cast as icons to the misery of man, were photographed from the superior view of the privileged class. Photographs are of the exceptional. Someone, somewhere thought that what was photographed was unique in some way and made an attempt to preserve an event, a place, a trick of light or simply the good feeling of the moment.

Photographs that are available to us today have gone through a series of selective editings. Those that survived basic natural selection – all things eventually rot – were first selected and saved by the photographer, later by his family or an archival institution. Ultimately, there is little logic invested in the saving or trashing of all of the billions of photographs that have been made.

AS MUCH AS OLD PHOTOGRAPHS CAN SHOW US how we have stayed the same, that we are an extension of the past, they can also indicate how we have changed. One of the most obvious differences is in our relationship with the landscape. Our ancestors, the Victorians considered themselves very much a part of the natural scheme of things, an integral part of nature. The concept of preservation was extant, as indicated by the formation of national parks, but nature was preserved for the use and appreciation of man. Few images of nature were made without a human figure, or some sign of human presence. As we progress into the twentieth century, fewer people appear in the image of the land. We have become an affront to nature, we no longer belong. Photographers carried on the classical, painterly tradition of the small figure in the landscape for a confusion of reasons. As a document, the human presence gave meaning to the event. As an image, the figure added to the composition and gave scale to what was considered a vast landscape. The human element also allowed the viewer to relate to an often hostile and alien environment in human terms.

In attempts to describe the effects of a photograph the medium has been likened to mirrors and windows, two words that evoke a sense of participation on the part of the viewer. When Oliver Wendell Holmes first used the phrase "mirror with a memory," he was in part referring to the shiny surface of the daguerreotype. The phrase has survived, however, through the ability of all photographs to reflect the viewer as part of what has gone before. Considered as windows, vintage photographs afford us the opportunity to indulge in the illicit thrills of cultural voyeurism, supplying flashes of recognition through the curtains of the past.

The superstition that photographs capture the soul of the subject is correct. Made by a master or through the attributes of serendipity, a powerful photograph can capture and transport the soul of both the subject and the viewer through time. Photographs are spells, bewitching the viewer; the image of a nation tugs at the heart like the image of an absent love. A love somewhere in time.

E.C.

Overleaf: British America, published in England by J & F. Tallis in 1851. From the Joe C.W. Armstrong Canadiana Collection.

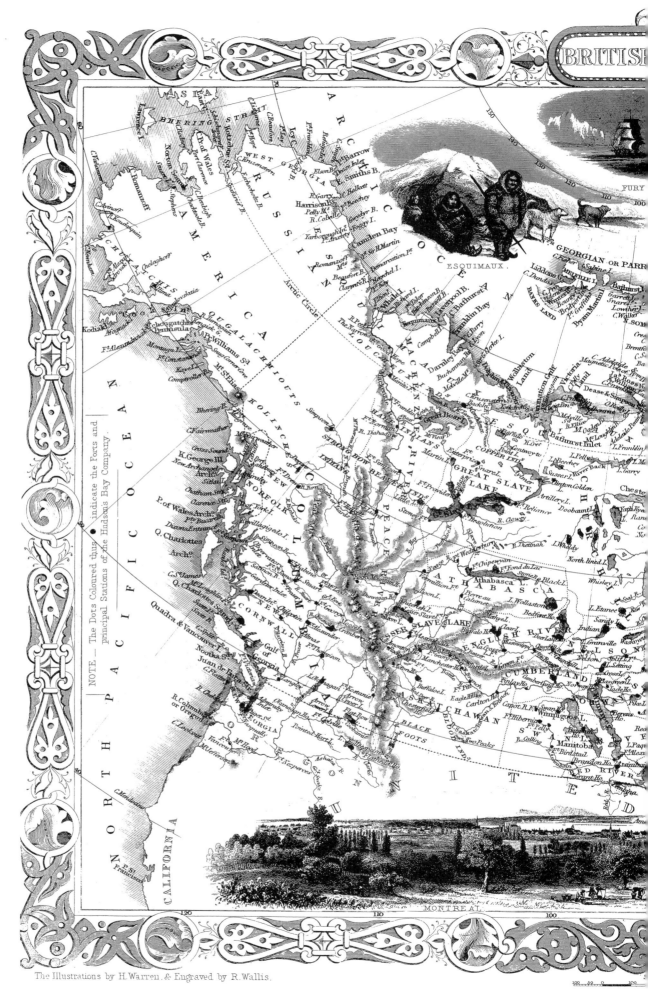

The Illustrations by H.Warren, & Engraved by R.Wallis.

J & F. TALLIS, LOND

AMERICA

The Map, Drawn & Engraved by J. Rapkin.

DINBURGH & DUBLIN.

SOMETIMES
A GREAT NATION
— Photo Album —

1. Maun-gua-daus, also known as George Henry, an Ojibwa Chief from the Port Credit area, c1847. One of the first photographs of a native Canadian, using the earliest photographic process, a daguerreotype.

2. "Breakfast in Hunters Camp," on the Blanche River, a tributary of the Ottawa River, Canada East (Quebec), c1865. Albumen print by Alexander Henderson (1831-1913), one of the most talented photographers working out of Montreal in the nineteenth century. The images he published in *Canadian Views and Studies, Photographed from Nature* are landscape classics.

No. 191.—VICTORIA BRIDGE, MONTREAL, CANADA.—ALONG THE TOP.

3. View along the top of Victoria Bridge, Montreal, Canada East (Quebec),
1859. An engineering triumph, the bridge was designed by the
British engineer Robert Stephenson and officially opened in 1860 by the
Prince of Wales. It was a vital link in the railway route connecting Toronto and
Montreal to the eastern seaboard of the United States. Hand-coloured, stereo
albumen print by English photographer William England for
the London Stereoscopic Company.

4. A.A. McCulloch dressed as an Indian (a recurring Canadian fascination)
for a fancy dress ball, c1863. Hand-coloured albumen print by William
Notman (1826-1891), the most famous and respected photographer of
Victorian Canada. William Notman's Montreal studio, established in 1856,
grew to become an international photo empire with branches throughout the
eastern United States and the Maritimes.

5. "Woman in the Trees," Moose Factory, James Bay, Rupert's Land (Ontario), c1865. In the 1860s a small group of Hudson's Bay Company employees at Moose Factory established what must have been one of the world's most remote camera clubs. Its members included the chief factor, James L. Cotter, a talented photographer whose work gained the attention of William Notman; the chief trader, Bernard Rogan Ross, who had a reputation as an anthropologist and naturalist; and Charles George Horetzky, an accountant who would later work as a photographer and surveyor in the search for a route for the Canadian Pacific Railway. Albumen print.

7. John A. Macdonald, Attorney General of Canada West (Ontario), 1857. Prime Minister of the Dominion of Canada from 1867-1873 and from 1878, to his death on June 6, 1891. Ambrotype.
Before the grave of him who, above all, was the father of Confederation, let not grief be barren grief. It may be said, without any exaggeration whatever, that the life of Sir John Macdonald...is the history of Canada....
Wilfrid Laurier, House of Commons, June 8, 1891.

6. The Centre Block of the Parliament Buildings, Ottawa, from the rear, featuring the Parliamentary Library, c1865. The library remains; the rest of the Centre Block was destroyed by fire in 1916. The original Parliament Buildings, built between 1859 and 1865, were designed by Thomas Fuller in the Gothic style called High Victorian; it was considered the Canadian national style in the late nineteenth century. This beautiful, large (39 x 52cm) albumen print is a relatively rare example of the use of oversize negatives in Canada. Photographed by Samuel McLaughlin (1826-1914), the official government photographist, 1861-93.

8. Group and carriage in the Annapolis Valley, Nova Scotia, c1855.
Ambrotype.

9. Tourist view of Niagara Falls, c1860. This full-plate (16.5 x 21.5 cm) ambrotype is one of the multitude made at the falls; the large size would have made it an expensive souvenir compared to the normal quarter-plate (8.3 x 10.5 cm) size.

10. Page from the Sewell family photo album, c1870. The dedication and patience focused on this illuminated photo collage is evidence of a time when the pace of life was slower and television was not the primary evening entertainment.

11. Children, c1860. Ambrotype.

12. The Gzowskis at the family home, The Hall, Toronto, c1857. Sir
Casimir Stanislaus Gzowski (1813-98) was born in Russia, son of a Polish
count, and came to Canada in 1841. An engineer and financier, he built the
Grand Trunk Railway from Toronto to Sarnia and in 1871-73 built the
International Bridge at Niagara Falls. He had five sons and three daughters.
Armstrong, Beere & Hime, salt print.

13. Rideau Falls, Ottawa, c1855. The buildings in the background are the
McKay & McKinnon cloth mill. Albumen print.

14. Montreal financier Andrew Robertson, c1864. Hand-coloured albumen
print by William Notman. The standard-sized *carte-de-visite* (10.5 x 6.5cm)
photograph was a fad imported from France in the late 1850s. The tiny,
immensely popular, portraits were an essential aspect of all Victorian photo
albums. Meant to be inexpensive, they were seldom in colour.

15. Bathing party at Murray Bay (La Malbaie) on the north shore of the St. Lawrence River, Quebec, c1875. Albumen print by Livernois & Bienvenue. The small community of Murray Bay was an exceptionally popular summering spot for the privileged class of Quebec and the Eastern United States and is still a quietly prestigious resort for some of the most influential families in North America.

16. Arch on Spring Garden Road, Halifax, Nova Scotia, built by General
Sir Charles Trollope, the British commander, in honour of the visit of the
Prince of Wales in 1860. The albumen print is by Wellington Chase,
considered one of the most important photographers in nineteenth-century
Halifax, where he was in business between 1855 and 1877. Building arches
was the quintessential expression of colonial loyalty. Lord Dufferin (Governor
General of Canada 1872-78) described some he had encountered
in a speech given in 1874:

There was an arch of cheeses, an arch of salt – an arch of
wheels, an arch of hardware, stoves, and pots and pans, an arch
of ladders laden with firemen in their picturesque costumes, an
arch of carriages, an arch of boats, a free trade arch, a
protectionist arch, an arch of children, and last of all, an arch –
no, not an arch, but rather a celestial rainbow of lovely ladies.

17. D'Arcy McGee (1825-1868) photographed in 1868. An expatriate Irish radical and eloquent apostle of Canadian unity, he was assassinated by a Fenian extremist on April 7, 1868. Salt print.

18. An unknown beauty, c1860. Ambrotype.

19. Shad fishing in the Jesus Rapids, Back River (Rivière des Prairies),
Montreal, c1865. William Notman, albumen print.

20. Timber coves near Quebec City, 1872. The square-timber trade in
Canadian white pine was beginning its decline when this picture was taken.
It had been given its biggest boost by Napoleon Bonaparte, who effectively
cut off the supply of Baltic timber to Britain in 1808. The Canadian trade
boomed and peaked about 1865, making square timbers a major export
commodity, along with furs, fish, flour and cheese. William Notman,
contemporary gelatine silver print.

21. Molson family brewery, Montreal, after the fire in 1858. Hand-coloured daguerreotype. The awkwardness of the process insured that there were relatively few full-plate daguerreotypes made outside the studio.

22. Herb Doctor, c1859. William Notman, hand-coloured, albumen print.

23. Chains dredged from Quebec City harbour during the summer of 1877.
Albumen print.

24. Drawing ice in Phillips Square, Montreal, c1870. Alexander Henderson, albumen print. Mechanical refrigeration was introduced in 1865 but river ice, cut and used in the winter or stored for the summer, was the main form of refrigeration until well into the twentieth century.

25. Quebec City, 1872. Stereo albumen print by Louis Prudent Vallée
(1837-1905), a Quebec City photographer who specialized in tourist views.

26. The European flavour of the Breakneck Steps, on Little Champlain
Street, made them one of Quebec City's most popular photographic scenes.
Stereo albumen print, 1865, by Ellisson and Co.

27. Pointe Lévi, Quebec, c1870. Alexander Henderson, albumen print.

28. "The Toboggan Party," Rideau Hall, Ottawa. This illuminated composite photograph produced by William James Topley in the 1870s is from Lady Dufferin's personal photo album. William Topley (1845-1930) opened the Ottawa studio for William Notman in 1867. He eventually purchased the business and went on to become one of Canada's leading photographers.

29. Ice cone, Montmorency Falls, near Quebec City, 1876. Albumen print
by Alexander Henderson. During the nineteenth century the Canadian
winter was a thing to be celebrated; Montmorency Falls became a popular
icon in paintings and photographs to the romantic vision of a frozen world.

31. Mrs. A.J. Corriveau's baby, 1878. William Notman, albumen print.

30. Skating in Victoria Rink, Montreal, 1881. William Notman was a master at creating these fantastic composite scenes. Each figure was individually posed in the studio, cut out, pasted onto a photographed or painted background, then rephotographed. The limitations of the photographic processes were overcome and an image created that would be purchased by all involved.

32. Tyne rowing crew, Lachine, Quebec, 1870. Taken before the day of easily produced "instantaneous views" this picture would have been carefully posed. William Notman, contemporary gelatine silver print.

33. Women workers sorting ore in the Huntington copper mine near Bolton, Quebec, 1867. This is a rare view of working conditions in mid-nineteenth-century Canada. William Notman, contemporary gelatine silver print.

34. Mrs. William Mackenzie, 1871. William Notman, albumen print.

35. Construction of the Intercolonial Railway, Smith Brook, Nova Scotia,
August 18, 1871. Albumen print.

36. Fort Chambly, Richelieu River, Quebec, 1863. The original fort was
built in 1665 by Captain Jacques de Chambly and named Fort St. Louis. It
was burned by the Iroquois in 1702. Rebuilt of stone and named Fort
Chambly in 1709-11; captured by the British in 1760 and the Americans in
1775 and again in 1812. Garrisoned until 1851, it was restored as an historic
site in 1921. William Notman, albumen print.

37. Retaining dam on the Blanche River, a tributary of the Ottawa River,
Quebec 1869. Alexander Henderson, albumen print.

38. Murray Bay, Quebec, c1868. Alexander Henderson, albumen print.

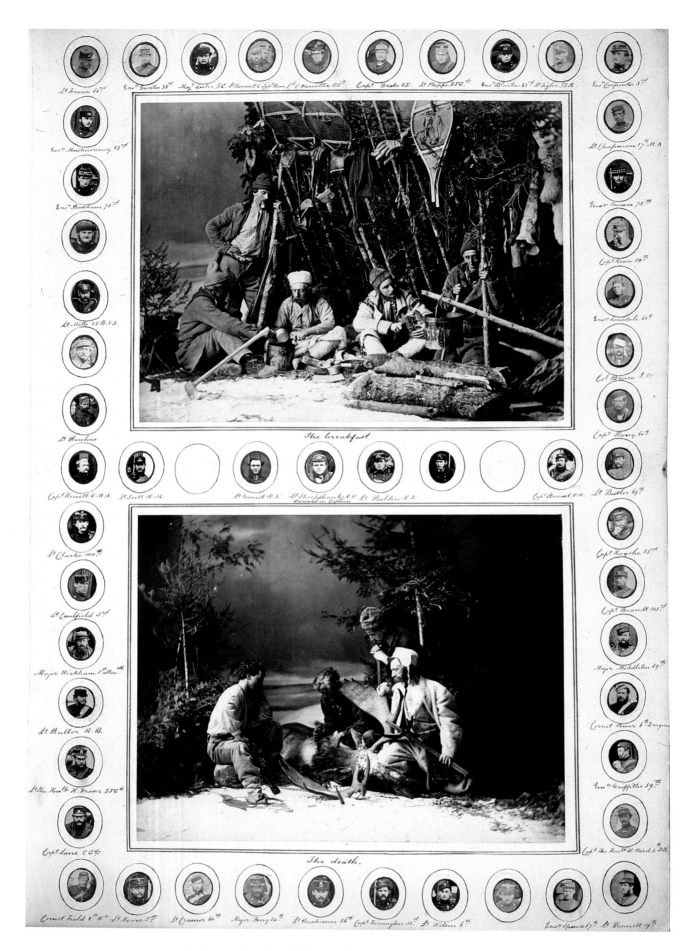

39. A page from Captain Thomas Grant's album, c1866. The two larger
prints are studio re-enactments by William Notman. The surrounding faces
are those of Captain Grant's fellow officers from the Royal School of
Musketry in Hythe, England. Grant retired from the British Army and
remained in Canada as an inspector of musketry for the Canadian Militia.
Albumen prints.

40. The object of the hunt, titled *A Thirsty Moose*, 1866. A studio creation by William Notman. These studio pictures were a source of particular pride for Notman and received universal acclaim. Outdoors, the vagaries of the climate and lighting, not to mention the difficulties of dealing with a real moose, would have interfered with the making of these rather stilted scenes. No effort was spared in bringing the outdoors inside.

41. The prairie on the banks of the Red River, September-October 1858.
The first photographs of the western interior of British North America were
made on the Assiniboine and Saskatchewan Exploring Expedition. The
photographer, Humphrey Lloyd Hime (1833-1903), used the cumbersome wet
collodion process that would remain the standard until the late 1880s. Hime
was a partner in Armstrong, Beere & Hime until about 1860, when he
became a successful member of the Toronto Stock Exchange.

42. Bodies of Crow Indians killed by the Peigans, found in the Sweetgrass
Hills by members of the British North America Boundary Survey, 1873.
Photographed by one of the Royal Engineer photographers, albumen print.
(Photography became a subject of instruction for the Royal Engineers in 1856.)

43. "The Hurdies," German dancing girls at the Cariboo goldfields, c1868. Frederick Dally, (1838-1914) the photographer, noted that there was "lots of elegant crinoline." Starting in 1858, goldseekers followed the Fraser River finds to the Cariboo district, where large deposits of gold were discovered in 1862. Dally opened his photographic studio in Victoria, B.C., in 1866 and another studio at Barkerville in the Cariboo in 1868. Before he left in 1870, Dally had produced many of the most notable images of the bustling colony. Albumen print.

44. Indian suspension bridge over the Wotsonqua (Bulkley) River at Hag-wilget Canyon, B.C., a few miles upstream from the junction of the Bulkley and Skeena rivers, 1872. The photographer, Charles George Horetzky (1838-1900), wanted to be known as a surveyor-explorer. He spent most of his adult life disagreeing with the powers that be over the route of the CPR. He had surveyed the northern route; the rails stayed south. Albumen print.

45. Still life on Vancouver Island. The photograph is from an album
belonging to Commander the Honourable Richard Hare entitled *Photographs
from the Cruise of HMS Myrmidon in the Pacific, 1873-1877.*
Illuminated albumen print.

46. Grave of a Couteaux chief near Lytton, B.C., 1867. The hides are from horses, mounts for the beyond. The pots and pans, also for use in the other world, were customarily punctured to remove temptation from those left behind. Frederick Dally, albumen print.

47. The residence of Guy Tuttle and family, Yale, B.C., c1870. A Hudson's
Bay Company post and trans-shipment point for the Cariboo goldfieds, Yale
lost its importance when the CPR line in the Fraser Canyon was completed
in 1885. Guy Tuttle was listed in the B.C. Directory for 1884 as proprietor of
the California House, a hostelry on Front Street. Attributed to Frederick
Dally, albumen print.

48. A Hannah Maynard studio fantasy, c1893. With her husband, Richard,
Hannah Maynard (1834-1918) established a photographic business in
Victoria, B.C. A spiritualist, she created many multiple-exposure images
involving herself, portraits of her dearly departed, and in this case her live
grandson, Maynard MacDonald. The technique was to make a series of
exposures on the same photographic plate using a mask over the lens to
prevent exposing the same area twice. Contemporary gelatine silver print.

49. Haida village of Yan, Queen Charlotte Islands, B.C., 1881, Edward
Dossetter. A professional photographer in Victoria, Dossetter accompanied
I.W. Powell, Superintendent of Indian Affairs for British Columbia, on a tour
of inspection along the coast aboard HMS *Rocket*. Albumen print.

Loading Ships at Moodyville. B.C.
By R. Maynard, Victoria, B.C.

MIRZAPORE

50. Loading lumber ships at Moodyville (North Vancouver), B.C., c1887.
Moodyville was named for Sewell Prescott Moody, who bought a sawmill in
1865 and gained timber rights to most of the north shore of Burrard Inlet.
The town was the most important in the area, with the first school on the
Inlet (1870) and first electric lights north of San Francisco (1882). Moodyville
was eclipsed by Vancouver in the 1880s. Richard Maynard (1832-1907),
albumen print.

52. A group of early members of the North West Mounted Police, who were fighting the whisky trade in the southern prairies, staged this drinking scene, probably at Fort Macleod, NWT (Alberta), c1879. Sergeant John A. Martin is second from left. The other Mounties are Sergeant M. J. Kirk, Corporal Crofton Uniacke and Constable Frederick Pope. Albumen print.

51. Freight wagons and machinery at Yale, B.C., c1868. Richard Maynard, albumen print.

53. William Ernest Losee and family, c1890. He was the owner of the first sawmill at Shawnigan Lake, Vancouver Island, B.C. The lumbermen in the background are standing on springboards; large trees were cut at that height to avoid difficult wide cuts and the rot that was common in the base. Jones and Company, albumen print.

54. Shipment leaving Hastings Mill, Vancouver, B.C., c1890. Baily Brothers
(Charles and William), a Vancouver photographic firm 1886 – 1919.
Gelatine silver print.

55. Native longshoremen and Chinese laundrymen at Moodyville (North
Vancouver), c1889. Albumen print.

56. Haida Indians, Masset, Queen Charlotte Islands, B.C., 1881, Edward
Dossetter, albumen print.

57. A pioneer bachelor's hall, Vancouver, 1890. Baily Brothers, gelatine silver print.

58. Ottertail bridge, CPR line, B.C., c1897. It was one of several mammoth trestles, hurriedly built of untreated timber as the railway was pushed through the mountains, that had to be replaced about ten years after construction. Platinotype print (platinum) by Richard H. Trueman (1856-1911). Trueman, in the portrait and view business in Vancouver from 1890 until 1911, was unique in his use of delicate and beautiful platinotype prints, a medium preferred by the photographic art community of the eastern United States.

70 OTTERTAIL BRIDGE. C.P.R.

R.H. TRUEMAN & CO., PHOTO., VANCOUVER, B. C.

59. Looking northeast from Idaho Mines, near Sandon, B.C., in the area of the West Kootenays that became known as the Silvery Slocan, c1895. About $100 million in ore was taken out of the region in its boom years around the turn of the century. Richard H. Trueman, Platinotype print.

60. Payne Bluff, a dramatic turning point on the Kaslo & Slocan Railway,
1900. The 29-mile line hauled ore from Sandon, B.C., to Kaslo on
Kootenay Lake; it also carried passengers, many of whom disembarked and
followed the train on foot around Payne Bluff. Richard H. Trueman,
platinotype print.

104. INDIAN SUN-DANCE, MAKING A BRAVE.

61. Blood Indian Sundance, July, 1887. William Hanson Boorne (1860-194-) was the only professional photographer permitted to photograph the ritual of placing ropes through the pectoral muscles before it was banned in the early 1890s. The endurance of pain was only a brief part of the Sundance, which could go on for several weeks. The ritual, performed by 15- or 16-year-old braves (usually for less than an hour), fulfilled a public vow made to the sun for sparing the dancer's life in a time of danger. Boorne was a commercial photographer in Calgary from 1886 to 1893 in the partnership Boorne & May. Albumen print.

KUYICOKOAN, SARCEE INDIAN.

62. "Otokuyicokoan, Sarcee Indian." Albumen print by William Hanson
Boorne, 1887. A dramatic change took place in photographing western
Indians after the completion of the railroad. Formerly photographed as filthy
savages, usually squatted on the ground, the Indians were now dressed in
their finery (occasionally an invention of the photographer) and hauled into a
studio replete with painted backdrop. No longer a threat to white society, the
Indians became romantic visions of a race thought doomed to extinction.
Albumen print.

63. Chief Piapot (second from right) and his headmen with
Lieutenant-Governor Edgar Dewdney (front, with white side whiskers) and
the Montreal Garrison Artillery, after the 1885 Northwest Rebellion. Oliver
B. Buell (1844-1910). "Professor Buell" was a noted lecturer and photographer hired by the CPR to make views along the newly constructed line.
Most of his best-known photographs were made during the aftermath of the
1885 Rebellion. Hand-coloured albumen print.

64. Bull Head, Sarcee Chief, by Alex J. Ross, Calgary, North West
Territories (Alberta), 1887. In 1884, Ross was a partner in Ross, Best & Co.
in Winnipeg. He established a studio in Calgary in 1886 and remained in
business until 1892. Hand-coloured albumen print.

65. Graveyard at Fort Qu'Appelle, NWT (Saskatchewan), 1885. O.B. Buell,
albumen print.

66. Regina, NWT (Saskatchewan), c1885. The Leader – the first newspaper
in the Territory of Assiniboia, was founded in 1883 by Nicholas Flood
Davin, who later became a member of Parliament. O.B. Buell,
albumen print.

67. Shackleton Brothers threshing outfit, NWT (Alberta), c1898. This picture was taken on the eve of the great explosion in prairie wheat production – from 17 million bushels in 1900 to 188 million by 1912. Photograph by Charles Wesley Mathers (1868-1950), who worked in the Edmonton branch of Boorne & May. He purchased their negatives when they went out of business in 1893 and, as was common practice, changed all the credit lines. His business was in turn purchased, in 1907, by Ernest Brown, who again changed all the credit lines. Consequently, Brown receives much of the credit for the work of his more talented predecessors. Gelatine silver print.

68. Round-up near Kamloops, c1895, by Stephen J. Thompson (1864-1930),
a photographer and publisher who worked out of New Westminster and
Vancouver from 1886 to 1914. Gelatine silver print.

69. Portage on the Smith Rapids, Slave River, NWT (Alberta) 1901,
C.W. Mathers. Gelatine silver print.

70. Last Chance Hotel, Yukon Territory, c1900. Gold was discovered at
Bonanza Creek in the Klondike in August, 1896. In the eight years that
followed, total value of gold production exceeded $100 million.
Gelatine silver print.

71. The Aurora Borealis, gelatine silver print attributed to Jerry Doody. Though one of the most striking features of the Canadian scene, the aurora was seldom photographed. Norwegian photographer Sophus Tromholt successfully photographed the northern lights in the early 1880s. This photograph, made in 1908 and showing the bright lights of Dawson, the capital of the Klondike Gold Rush, may be the first successful Canadian attempt.

72. Palace Grand Theatre, Dawson, Yukon Territory, c1900. Constructed
from the remains of two steamboats, it represented a new level of
sophistication for the gold rush pleasure centre, according to Pierre Berton.
Gelatine silver print.

73. Klondike Kate (Kate Rockwell), 1900. The immensely popular American
dancer left the Yukon with Alexander Pantages, a Greek waiter who weighed
the miners' gold at the Monte Carlo Dance Hall and Saloon in Dawson.
Using his own take from the saloon's patrons and Kate's considerable
earnings, Pantages went on to establish a theatre chain in the United States
and Canada. He made a fortune and dropped Kate for a 17-year-old bride.
Kate went on to three husbands and died in 1957.

74. James Croil and Party, 1888. A Scot who came to Canada in the 1840s, Croil was the owner of Crysler's Farm, site of a famous battle in the War of 1812, and became an official of the Presbyterian Church in Canada and editor of the Presbyterian Record. The author of books on a variety of subjects, he travelled widely in North America, Europe, Russia and Japan. William Notman & Son, contemporary gelatine silver print.

75. Montreal Harbour, c1875. William Notman, albumen print.

76. St. Catherine Street, main street of Canada's largest city, Montreal, in
1901. William Notman & Son, gelatine silver print.

77. Skiing at Rockcliffe Park, Ottawa, 1895. Lord Frederick Hamilton,
aide-de-camp to the Governor General, Lord Lansdowne, introduced the
sport to Ottawa in 1887. He was greeted by universal derision when he tried
the slopes of Rockcliffe Park, near the Governor General's residence, Rideau
Hall. William James Topley, gelatine silver print.

78. Flood in the Bonaventure depot, Montreal, 1886. The annual spring
flood was a persistent feature of life in Montreal. In particularly bad years
some of the citizens would "borrow" planks from the wooden sidewalks to
raft their way home. Albumen print by George Charles Arless (1864-1903),
one of the many photographers trained in the Notman studios who
established his own photographic business.

79. The summer home of Charles Gurd, a manufacturer of soft drinks, near Montreal, c1886. William Notman & Son, contemporary gelatine silver print.

80. Pauline Johnson (1862-1913). The poet, also known by her Indian name
Tekahionwake, was born near Brantford, Ontario, the daughter of an English-
woman and a Mohawk chief. Gelatine silver print by Cochran, c1895.

By right, by birth we Indians own these lands,
Though starved, crushed, plundered, lies our nation low...
Perhaps the white man's God has willed it so.

81. Parliament Buildings, Ottawa 1875. Albumen print, William Notman.

Marjorie H. Gordon — "The Forests of Canada."
1898.

82. Lady Marjorie Gordon, daughter of the Governor General, Lord
Aberdeen. Her costume for a fancy dress ball in 1898 was designed to represent "The Forests of Canada." William James Topley, gelatine silver print.

83. Rear view of the Perley & Pattee sawmill, Ottawa, 1872. One of the
Fathers of Confederation, John Hamilton Gray, recalled the coming of the
lumber barons and industrial promoters like Bronson, Pattee and Perley,
Harris and Eddy, in his book on Confederation, published in 1872:

> The river was put in harness; and now the spot, which at
> that time was simply known as a scene of beauty, is crowded
> with mills and machine shops, and, including both sides of
> the Falls, affords unceasing employment to twenty thousand
> people, daily creating untold wealth....
> William Notman, albumen print.

84. Steam drilling at the Silver Lake Mine, in Eastern Ontario, c1908.
H.N. Topley (1849-1908), gelatine silver print.

85. Interior of the centre dome, Portsmouth Penitentiary, Kingston, Ontario, c1890. The prison was built in 1835, in the small community of Portsmouth. The town was later amalgamated with Kingston. Gelatine silver print.

86. Bay Street, from the east side looking south, after the Toronto fire of
April 19, 1904; 122 buildings on 14 acres of land were destroyed leaving 5,000
people temporarily out of work. The city resolved to upgrade the water mains
to increase the pressure. Henry F. Sharpe, gelatine silver print. Sharpe
operated one of the leading photographic supply companies in Canada.

87. A peninsula before a series of storms in 1858, the Toronto Islands have been a popular summer resort since the peninsular days when Louis Privat's hotel offered a "menagerie, bowling alleys and good fare." Stereo view, 1894, by Benjamin West Kilburn, one of the largest American manufacturers of stereo views. Gelatine silver print.

"The Knapp Roller Boat And Its Inventor."

By WILLIAM THOMSON FREELAND, Official Artist and Photographer, 143 College St., Toronto, Ont.

Invented by F. A. KNAPP, B.C.L., of Prescott, Ont., the boat was financed by GEO. GOODWIN, of Ottawa, Ont.

(Portraits, etc., Finished in Oil and Water Colors, Pastel, Crayon, etc.)

The Contractors were the POLSON IRON WORKS of Toronto, Ont., and the Supervisor, W. E. REDWAY, M.I.N.A., of London, Eng.

The above picture of the Marine Roller, represents it as it appeared in Toronto Bay, October 27th, 1897, on a preliminary trial. The vessel is an annular cylinder, 110 feet long and 22 feet in diameter, with a space of 3 feet between the inner and outer shells, which space is divided into water-tight compartments. Near the ends, the outer shell, upon which are placed the paddles, tapers to 12 feet in diameter, forming the cone ends. The engines, two in each end, run upon tracks riveted to the inside of the outer shell, the continuity of the inner shell being broken so as to allow the machinery to work at the greatest distance from the centre, thereby gaining the greatest leverage. The progress of the engines, like the squirrel in its cage, causes the boat to roll. The rudders, one at each end of the boat, are placed under the bridges which are rigid to the trucks of the engines. This is merely an experimental model of an ocean vessel to be built feet long and 200 feet in diameter, inside which from central bearings will be suspended three separate cylindrical vessels or compartments. In the middle one of these having the greatest diameter, the motive power, developed from engines resting on its bottom, will be applied by ordinary crank action to a central shaft rigid by means of spokes to the outer shells or revolving portion of the boat through openings in which the smoke and exhaust steam from the engines will escape. In the other compartments, with their bottoms 40 feet above sea level, will be laid the decks, the uppermost of which will be 100 feet above sea level, and over these the upper halves of the compartments will form arched roofs 60 feet high. As the outer ends above the highest decks will be open ample light and ventilation will be obtained; also owing to the suspension of the decks, all disagreeable motion will be eliminated. This vessel, unlike the present type of ships, rolls over instead of ploughing through the water against the resistance of skin friction and the vastly greater retardation caused by the pressure of the water at the bow. The Roller as it increases its speed, utilizes this resistance, which also increases, but in a vastly greater proportion, to rise to the surface of the water until this resistance equals the weight of the boat, when she must roll on top of the water. The inventor claims that now, that the soundness of the principle has been demonstrated, and all that remains to be solved is in the nature of details, which can be easily worked out, he will, with his larger vessel, be able to attain a speed of at least one mile a minute, and with much greater comfort and safety than the best of the present type of ships can give. It is now proposed to build a boat, according to this latter plan, of sufficient size to cross the Atlantic, and which, after trial, will furnish accurately the data required to determine whether any modifications will be found necessary. When this has been successfully accomplished a Joint Stock Company will be formed called the "Knapp Ocean Navigation Company, Limited," when boats of the largest dimensions will be built and put into service.—F. A. KNAPP.

Entered according to Act of the Parliament of Canada in the year 1898, by W. T. FREELAND, at the Department of Agriculture.　　Entered according to Act of Congress, in the year 1898, by W. T. FREELAND, in the Office of the Librarian of Congress at Washington.

88. The Knapp Roller Boat, 1897. Gelatine silver print.

89. Tourists at Niagara Falls, c1890. Albumen print.

90. Clifford M. Calverley, one of the many stuntmen of Niagara Falls, running his wheelbarrow over the wire, Whirlpool Rapids, c1895. The Toronto Daredevil made his first crossing on October 12, 1892. On one of these trips he set a speed record for crossing the wire of 2 minutes and 32 seconds. Underwood & Underwood, stereo gelatine silver print.

91. Painting a diorama of the Gaspé area for the new Victoria Memorial Museum, Ottawa, April 1913. Gelatine silver print.

92. Rocher Percé, Gaspé, Quebec c1905. William Notman & Son,
gelatine silver print.

93. Murray Bay, Quebec, 1900. William Notman & Son, albumen print.

94. Rustico Beach, Prince Edward Island, c1916. William Notman & Son, contemporary gelatine silver print.

95. Clearing a log jam, Ontario, c1890. Gelatine silver print.

96. Log jam, Grand Falls, New Brunswick, c1890. Gelatine silver print.

97. Bridges over the Reversing Falls, Saint John, N.B., c1898. At low tide, the flow of the St. John River drops 17 feet at this point. Due to the extreme tides in the Bay of Fundy, the water flow is reversed at high tide, creating a reversing falls – and a very popular tourist experience. William Notman & Son, gelatine silver print.

98. Workmen with a carved Atlantic (harbour) salmon for the spire of
Trinity Church, Saint John, N.B., c1910. Contemporary gelatine silver print
by Isaac Erb (1846-1939). Primarily an industrial photographer, Erb took
pictures throughout the Maritimes after establishing his studio in Saint John
in the late 1870s.

99. Laying a macadam road surface (early asphalt, named for the Scottish
inventor J.L. McAdam), Mount Pleasant Avenue, Saint John, N.B., c1900.
Isaac Erb, contemporary gelatine silver print.

100. Odevaine family and friends at York Redoubt, a remnant of the
Imperial presence near Halifax, August 1898. Amateur snapshot,
gelatine silver print.

101. A member of the Albert No. 2 fire-engine company, Halifax, c1870.
Parish & Co. photograph, coloured albumen print.

102. Hopewell Cape, Bay of Fundy, N.B., c1900. The tradition of the small
figure in the landscape was pervasive in nineteenth-century Canadian
photography. Even if the intent was simply to give scale to the scene, the
tradition provided an eminently human record of an overwhelming
landscape. William Notman & Son, gelatine silver print.

103. Lily pond near Kentville, Nova Scotia c1896. Amos Lawson Hardy
(1860-1935), gelatine silver print.

104. Group and Stanley Steamer, Kentville, N.S., c1902. The car was made
by the Stanley twins, who abandoned a profitable photographic plate
business to become the first real mass producers of cars in the United States.
At least eight Canadian car companies had been in business by 1902,
including one at Hopewell, N.S. Hand-coloured gelatine silver print.

105. Steel mill at North Sydney, Cape Breton Island, N.S., c1904. The Island, which yielded both coal and limestone, got its first pig iron and steel furnaces in 1900. Isaac Erb, gelatine silver print.

106. A victim of the fire, 1897, Windsor, N.S. Ninety percent of the town was destroyed, leaving over 2,000 people homeless. There were disastrous fires in many other Canadian centres in the nineteenth century; wood construction, lack of building clearance and token firefighting equipment were factors contributing to the devastation. Gelatine silver print.

107. Marconi's towers at Table Head, Glace Bay, Cape Breton Island, c1904. The Italian inventor Guglielmo Marconi (1874-1937) perfected wireless transmission when he bridged the English Channel by wireless in 1898. In 1901 the first trans-Atlantic signal (three dots for the letter S) was transmitted from Europe and received at Signal Hill, St. John's, Newfoundland. In 1902 Marconi established regular wireless communication with Europe from these towers at Glace Bay. Isaac Erb, gelatine silver print.

108. H.D. Reid's automobile in front of the Cabot Tower at Signal Hill,
St. John's, Newfoundland. 1908. Harry Reid was a son of Sir Robert Reid
(1842-1908), who built the Newfoundland, Railway. In return he was given
one-ninth of the entire island of Newfoundland.
William Notman & Son, gelatine silver print.

109. J. Savage with "the guns used in firing the Royal Salute" during the
visit of the Duke and Duchess of Cornwall and York in 1901, St. John's.
James Vey, gelatine silver print.

110. Jigging for squid in Burin, southeast coast of Newfoundland, c1900.
Robert E. Holloway, gelatine silver print.

111. Pouch Cove, Newfoundland, 1900. Robert E. Holloway (1850-1904),
gelatine silver print.

112. Under the cod drying flakes, near St. John's, 1880. Flakes were a
familiar sight in all Newfoundland fishing communities; the latticed platforms
allowed the air to preserve the catch in the period before refrigeration.
Simeon H. Parsons (c1844-1908) was one of the first photographers in
Newfoundland. Albumen print.

113. Sealers copying the floes, c1920. Copying is a Newfoundland term for leaping from floe to floe. Sealing was perilous; in 1914, 77 men from the sealer *Newfoundland* froze to death when they were left on the ice overnight. The same year all 173 aboard the *Southern Cross* perished when the sealer capsized. R.E. Holloway, gelatine silver print.

114. The *Arctic* at Port Burwell, Ungava (Quebec) across Hudson Strait from Baffin Island, September 1907. The ship, commanded by Captain J.E. Bernier, was returning from an expedition to take possession of the Arctic islands in the name of Canada. George R. Lancefield, gelatine silver print.

115. She-nuck-shoo, Eskimo chief, Cape Fullerton, Hudson Bay, 1905-06. A portrait taken by Geraldine Moodie (1853-1945), a professional photographer who accompanied her husband, Major J.D. Moodie, on the Canadian Arctic Patrol, which was commissioned to establish posts for the North West Mounted Police. Gelatine silver print.

116. Koo-tuck-tuck, deaf-mute Eskimo girl, Cape Fullerton, Hudson Bay
1905-06. Geraldine Moodie, gelatine silver print.

117. Kayak in floes 1920-21 (probably at Cape Dufferin, Hudson Bay). A gravure print of a photograph made by Robert Flaherty (1884-1951) during the filming of his most famous movie, *Nanook of the North*. Flaherty wished to illustrate the "former majesty of primitive peoples."

118. HMS *Discovery,* one of two ships of the British Arctic Expedition under
the command of Captain George S. Nares, in winter quarters, Ellesmere
Island, Latitude 81°44' N, 1875-76. Nares's ship, HMS *Alert,* got to
82°28'N, the highest latitude reached by any ship to that date. Exploration
parties of the expedition, the last British naval attempt to reach the North
Pole, attained 83°20'26". The structures in the foreground are the smithy
and the theatre. Thomas Mitchell, paymaster of the *Discovery,* was also
trained as a photographer at the Royal Engineers school at Chatham; he used
the wet collodion process and an albumen-beer dry plate process to photograph in temperatures that reached -64°F. Albumen print.

A VIEW SHEWING TOPEK . KAYAK & ESKIMO   278   PHOTO BY C.W. MATHERS EDMONTON

119. Topek (summer house), Kayak and Eskimo, Peel River, NWT, 1901.
CW. Mathers, gelatine silver print.

120. Elliott Barnes (1866-1938) in his cabin on the Kootenay Plains, Alberta, 1907. Barnes was a guide, rancher, and occasionally a professional photographer. He often used himself (as in this self-portrait) or his family as models to portray a very romantic wilderness lifestyle. Contemporary gelatine silver print.

121. Western Anemone, by Mary M. Vaux, c1910. Mary Vaux (1860-1940) was a member of a family of Philadelphians who dedicated themselves to the study of the Canadian Rockies. Among her achievements was *North American Wildflowers*, a five-volume, limited-edition portfolio of her flower paintings, published by the Smithsonian Institution. Hand-coloured lantern slide.

122. Sampson Beaver and family, Stoney Indians, Kootenay Plains, Alberta, 1906. Photograph by Mary T.S. Schäffer (1861-1939), an author, naturalist, photographer and explorer. Contemporary gelatine silver print.

123. Oscar Barnes, with his daughter, Lois, at Sawback Lake, Banff National
Park, taken by his son, Elliott, in the period 1906-08.
Contemporary gelatine silver print.

124. Mount Temple in cloud, from Ptarmigan Valley, Banff National Park, 1906. Platinum print by the Vaux Family (Mary Vaux and her brothers, George and William).

125. Alpine Club of Canada members on the summit horn of Mount Resplendent, Mount Robson area, B.C., 1913. The photographer, Byron Harmon (1876-1942), had made the first ascent of the 11,240-foot peak in 1911 with guide Conrad Kain. Harmon, who established a postcard and view business in Banff in 1903, became the premier mountain photographer in Canada. Contemporary gelatine silver print.

126. Bow Lake, Banff National Park, Alberta, 1924. Byron Harmon,
coloured gelatine silver print.

127. T.H. Beach, a rancher near Gleichen, Alberta, c1910. Hand-coloured gelatine silver print.

128. The first oil boom in Calgary following the 1914 discovery of oil
in Turner Valley just south of the city. Harry Pollard (1880-1968) had a
photographic business in Calgary from 1899 to 1924. He then joined
Associated Screen News and travelled the world photographing for the CPR.
Contemporary gelatine silver print.

130. Model T Ford at Eastburg, Alberta, c1920. Contemporary
gelatine silver print.

129. J.W. Millar celebrating his hemp crop at North Battleford,
Saskatchewan, 1920. Harry Pollard, contemporary gelatine silver print.

131. Marrows shown by Lillie Reeves, Edmonton, Alberta, 1907. Ernest
Brown (1877-1951). Contemporary gelatine silver print.

132. Apples, Kentville, Nova Scotia, 1911. Amos Lawson Hardy.
Gelatine silver print.

133. Vegetables from D. Ross's garden, Edmonton, NWT, 1902. Mr. Ross's garden was used frequently to illustrate, beyond any doubt, the fertility of the Canadian West. C.W. Mathers, gelatine silver print.

134. An advertisement for McClary stoves, 1897. Gelatine silver print.

135. Canadian Postcard Company, c1912. Gelatine silver print.

136. Timber wolves killed by George Ross during a day's hunt along the Little Bow River southeast of Calgary, c1893. Heads mounted by Walker McKay. Photograph by William Hanson Boorne, albumen print.

137. Four days' hunt at the Lake of the Woods, Ontario, 1913. C.G. Linde,
gelatine silver print.

138. Wrestling with a trained bear, c1902. Gelatine silver print.

Where in the early springtime
the crocus spreads a gorgeous mantle o'er the prairie
G.S. Hunter's homestead, Sask. Apr. 10th 1910

139. Photograph by William M. Tegart (1862-1921), a professional
photographer in Lumsden, Saskatchewan. Gelatine silver print, 1910.

140. Rock pillars in No. 1 tunnel level, Granby Mine, Phoenix, B.C., c1905.
It was one of several mining sites in the province for one of Canada's major
copper producers, Granby Consolidated Mining, Smelting and Power
Company. Gelatine silver print.

141. Reserve Mine, Western Fuel Corporation of Canada, Nanaimo, B.C.,
c1920. The Hudson's Bay Company opened the coalfields at Nanaimo in
1852; English and Scottish miners were brought in and the mines lasted for a
century. The belching smokestacks symbolized the payroll for the militant
British Columbia labour movement and for one of the great Canadian
fortunes belonging to Robert Dunsmuir, son of an Ayrshire coal master who
emigrated to Vancouver Island in 1851. Gelatine silver print.

ENTERED ACCORDING
TO ACT OF THE PARLIAMENT OF CANADA IN THE YEAR 1903, BY EDWARDS BROS.
VANCOUVER, B. C., AT THE DEPARTMENT OF AGRICULTURE.
5103

142. Salmon Fishing, British Columbia, 1903. The first Pacific salmon
cannery was built at Annieville on the Fraser River in 1870; provincial
production totalled 473,674 cases in 1903 and the salmon can had become a
symbol of Canada, as obvious as the Rocky Mountains. Edwards Brothers
(George William and Edgar Herbert), gelatine silver print.

143. Unidentified portrait, probably on Vancouver Island, B.C., c1905.
Cyanotype print.

144. Stanley Park, Vancouver, B.C., c1908. Four-colour lithograph.

145. Woman costumed by H.M. Murray, the Canadian Government agent
in Exeter, England, to advertise Canadian prosperity in a parade, 1907.
T.A. Chandler, gelatine silver print.

146. Celebration, southern Ontario, c1906. The photographs of William James (1866-1948), an extremely active and talented Toronto freelance photojournalist, captured the spark of life. Gelatine silver print.

147. George H. Hees and his wife at the Ontario Jockey Club, c1911. A
manufacturer of window blinds, among other things, he was the grandfather
of George Hees, a cabinet minister in the Diefenbaker government.
William James, gelatine silver print.

148. Motorcade for Sir Wilfrid Laurier electioneering in Simcoe, Ontario, in 1911. He campaigned on the reciprocity issue (free trade with the United States) and lost to the Conservatives. Gelatine silver print.

149. Hitch-hikers in Muddy York (Toronto), c1907. William James,
gelatine silver print.

150. Steam hammer, Toronto, c1910. William James, gelatine silver print.

151. Carving an Ionic capital during construction of the Legislative
Building, Winnipeg, 1915. A triumph of neo-classic design, the building was
opened in 1920 when Winnipeg was in decline following one of
the most extraordinary booms in Canadian history. Foote & James photo,
gelatine silver print.

TWO FIRST MEN ACROSS C P RY VIADUCT
LETHBRIDGE ALTA

152. The CPR's Lethbridge Viaduct across the Oldman River in Alberta, 1909. Over a mile long and 314 feet high, it's the longest and highest railway bridge in Canada. One wonders how often they had to jump the gap to get the photograph right. Gelatine silver print.

153. The Quebec Bridge, being built by a U.S. firm, lies in the river
after a span fell on August 29, 1907, killing 75 men. The centre span of
the second bridge, on which work began in 1911, fell September 11, 1916,
while being hoisted into position; 13 men died. The bridge was completed in 1917. Gelatine silver print from the Dominion Bridge collection.

154. A 145-ton link for the top of the main post of the second Quebec
Bridge in the St. Lawrence Bridge Company shops, Montreal, 1915. Eugene
Michael Finn (1880-1959). The official photographer for the second bridge
construction, Finn made some of the finest engineering photographs in
Canada. Gelatine silver print.

156. After the fire at the Kelly Block, Bannatyne Avenue, Winnipeg, January 1911. Lewis B. Foote (1873-1957) was a commercial photographer in Winnipeg from 1902 to 1948 (from 1907 to 1928 he was in partnership with George James). Contemporary gelatine silver print.

155. Waterfront at the Canadian National Exhibition grounds, Toronto, c1909. William James, gelatine silver print.

157. The fresh-air cure for tuberculosis, Toronto, September 6, 1912. The cot and umbrella were supplied for the boy after he refused sanitarium care. He died later at Weston Sanitarium. Arthur Goss (1881-1940) was the City of Toronto's official photographer from 1911 to 1940; in that capacity he created a stark document of urban living conditions. Gelatine silver print.

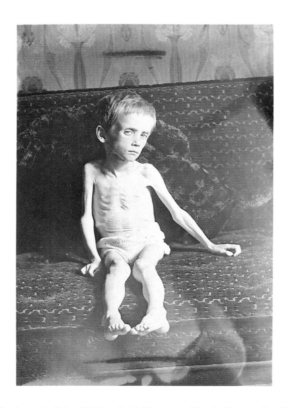

158. A ward of the Children's Aid Society of Perth County, Stratford, Ontario, c1895. This photograph is in the collection of John Joseph Kelso, who arrived in Toronto from Ireland as a 10-year-old in 1874 and became one of the leading figures in the introduction of child-care programs in Canada. By Stratford photographer Young Shannon, gelatine silver print.

159. Children in "The Ward," an inner-city enclave in Toronto
that became home for many immigrant families, c1908. William James,
gelatine silver print.

160. One of a series of portraits of children and animals made by Reuben R. Sallows (1855-1937), Goderich, Ontario, c1910. Gelatine silver print.

161. Unidentified child, c1910, William James, hand-coloured lantern slide

Within the photograph: PARKS 515 MAY 28 1915 SENIOR BASEBALL OPENING RIVERDALE

162. Senior baseball, Riverdale, Toronto, May 22, 1915.
Gelatine silver print.

163. Roy Campbell (on right, the winner) vs Dick Hyland, representing the communities of Brighouse and Steveston, May 3, 1913, Vancouver, B.C. W.J. Cairns, gelatine silver print.

164. "Baddeck No. 1" built by the Canadian Aerodrome Company, undergoing military trials, Petawawa, Ontario, August 1909. The first "all Canadian" aircraft, it was designed, built and flown by F. W. (Casey) Baldwin and J.A.D. McCurdy. Gelatine siver print.

165. Performer at the Canadian National Exhibition, Toronto, c1912. The
CNE was first held in 1878, an outgrowth of the Toronto Exhibition that
started in 1846. William James, gelatine silver print.

166. Dr. Margaret Patterson (1875-1962) exhibiting a cow in a Toronto park as part of the pure milk campaign, c1914. Once a medical missionary to India, Dr. Patterson was acutely aware of the dangers of unpasteurized milk which resulted in brucellosis, a potentially fatal disease that is virtually unknown today. Gelatine silver print.

167. Diving Horse, Hanlan's Point, Toronto Island, c1908. One of the more
sensational carnival acts at the turn of the century. William James, gelatine
silver print.

168. Unidentified bridal party, Toronto, c1910. William James,
hand-coloured lantern slide.

169. Miss F. Billings and friends, Montreal, 1915. William Notman & Son, contemporary gelatine silver print.

170. Off to war, Toronto, 1916. William James, gelatine sliver print.

171. Military guard on the Quebec Bridge, 1916. The guard was a wartime
precaution against sabotage. Eugene Michael Finn, gelatine silver print.

172. War production at the Canadian Linderman Company, Woodstock,
Ontario, 1918. Gelatine silver print.

173. Campbell Road, after the Halifax Explosion of December 6, 1917. A munitions ship and a relief ship collided in Halifax Harbour, and more than 1,600 people died in the resulting explosion. Gelatine silver print.

174. Trench warfare demonstration, Toronto, c1914.
William James, gelatine silver print.

175. Demonstrating the newest weapon of war on University Avenue,
Toronto, Armistice Day, 1918. William James, gelatine silver print.

176. Canadian troops in France, 1914 – 1918. Over 60,000 Canadians died
in the "War to End All Wars."

177. The troopship *Olympic* (sister ship to the *Titanic*) in dazzle paint,
Halifax, 1919. Completed in 1911, the four-funnelled *Leo Olympic* was
scrapped in 1937. British and Colonial Press, gelatine silver print.

178. Returning troops, Halifax, 1919. British and Colonial Press,
gelatine silver print.

179. Riding demonstration, CNE, Toronto, c1920. William James,
hand-coloured lantern slide.

180. The Royal North West Mounted Police on Main Street, returning after the third charge on "Bloody Saturday," June 21, 1919, during the Winnipeg General Strike. Two people were killed and twenty injured. The strike reflected the conflict between the old craft unions and the new militant industrial groups exemplified by the One Big Union, founded in Calgary in March that year. The strike, which began on May 15, collapsed on June 26. Photograph by British and Colonial Press Limited, gelatine silver print.

181. "Imperial Kouncil of the Kanadian Knights of the Ku Klux Klan" in front of their Imperial Palace, Glen Brae, on Matthews Avenue, Vancouver, November 1925. The Klansmen were not restricted to Vancouver; they were active all across Canada. Stuart Thomson (1881-1960) was a commercial photographer whose business slogan was "anything, anywhere, anytime." Contemporary gelatine silver print.

182. Speed skaters, championship meet, 1924. William James, hand-coloured
lantern slide.

184. Demonstrating a radiophone, Edmonton, July 14, 1922. The gentleman has a crystal radio in his ring. The most basic receiver, a crystal of galena or molybdenite, can pick up radio signals and generate a weak signal in the earphone. Commercial broadcasting began in North America in 1920. Frederick McDermid, contemporary gelatine silver print.

183. Crowd watching a Human Fly, King Street, Toronto, c1920. William James, gelatine silver print.

185. Ferris wheels, Canadian National Exhibition, Toronto, 1924.
William James, gelatine silver print.

186. Foul Bay beach and Gonzales Heights, Victoria, B.C., c1920. Gus A.
Maves (1882-1942), one of the finest colourists in Canada, was a
photographer in Toronto for 17 years before moving to Victoria in 1918.
Hand-coloured lantern slide.

187. Getting greased for a marathon swim in Lake Ontario in the 1920s.
The Wrigley chewing gum company put up the prize money (a total purse of
$50,000) for the first marathon swim at the Canadian National Exhibition in
1927. The 21-mile swim in Lake Ontario was billed as the greatest aquatic
event in history. William James, hand-coloured lantern slide.

188. The Prince of Wales (who abdicated in 1936 before being crowned Edward VIII) with his brother Prince George, later Duke of Kent, in Winnipeg, 1927. Lewis B. Foote, contemporary silver print.

189. Poultry class at Olds College, Olds, Alberta, 1921. Frederick McDermid
Studio, gelatine silver print.

190. Strawberry pickers, Gordon Head, Vancouver Island, B.C., c1920.
Gus A. Maves. Hand-coloured lantern slide.

191. Hand-coloured lantern slide used in theatre presentations, 1912.

List of Plates

Frontispiece:
William Armstrong and William Napier
Armstrong, Beere & Hime 1858
Collection: Whyte Museum of the Canadian
Rockies, Banff

1. Maun-gua-daus (George Henry), Ojibwa Chief
c1847
Collection: Public Archives of Canada, Ottawa,
PA125840(NPC-55)

2. "Breakfast in Hunters Camp"
Alexander Henderson c1865
Collection: Ontario Archives, Toronto

3. Victoria Bridge, Montreal, Canada East
(Quebec)
William England 1859
Collection: the author

4. A.A. McCulloch dressed as an Indian
William Notman c1863
Collection: Notman Photographic Archives,
McCord Museum, Montreal

5. "Woman in the Trees," James Bay, Rupert's
Land (Ontario)
c1865
Collection: Ontario Archives, Toronto

6. The Parliamentary Library, Ottawa, Canada
West (Ontario)
Samuel McLaughlin c1865
Collection: Public Archives of Canada, Ottawa,
C-18371 (NPC-35)

7. John A. Macdonald
1857
Collection: Public Archives of Canada, Ottawa,
C 4145 (NPC-33)

8. Group and carriage, Annapolis Valley,
Nova Scotia
c1855
Collection: Nova Scotia Museum, Halifax,
P9576.33.1

9. Niagara Falls, Canada West (Ontario)
c1860
Collection: Ontario Archives, Toronto

10. Page from the Sewell family album
c1870
Collection: National Gallery of Canada
P81:003:14

11. Children
c1860
Collection: National Gallery of Canada, Ottawa,
P72:001:19, Ralph Greenhill Collection

12. Gzowski family at The Hall, Toronto,
Canada West (Ontario)
Armstrong, Beere & Hime c1857
Collection: Ontario Archives, Toronto

13. Rideau Falls, Ottawa, Canada West (Ontario)
c1855
Collection: Public Archives of Canada, Ottawa,
C-3853 (NPC-1)

14. Andrew Robertson
William Notman c1864
Collection: Notman Photographic Archives,
McCord Museum, Montreal

15. Bathing party at Murray Bay, Quebec
Livernois & Bienvenue c1875
Collection: Notman Photographic Archives,
McCord Museum, Montreal

16. General Trollope's arch, Halifax, Nova Scotia
Wellington Chase 1860
Collection: Public Archives of Nova Scotia,
Halifax, N 1253

17. D'Arcy McGee
1868
Collection: Public Archives of Canada, Ottawa,
C-21543 (NPC-45)

18. An unknown beauty
c1860
Collection: Public Archives of Canada, Ottawa
(NPC-50)

19. Shad fishing near Montreal, Canada East
(Quebec)
William Notman c1865
Collection: Ed McCann, Regina

20. Timber coves near Quebec City, Quebec
William Notman 1872
Collection: Notman Photographic Archives,
McCord Museum, Montreal

21. Molson family brewery, after the fire,
Montreal, Canada East (Quebec)
1858
Collection: Public Archives of Canada, Ottawa
C-89689 (NPC-32)

22. Herb Doctor
William Notman c1859
Collection: Ontario Archives, Toronto

23. Chains dredged from Quebec City harbour,
Quebec
1877
Collection: Public Archives of Canada, Ottawa,
C-3999 (NPC-29)

24. Drawing ice, Montreal, Canada East
(Quebec)
Alexander Henderson c1870
Collection: Notman Photographic Archives,
McCord Museum, Montreal

25. Quebec City, Quebec
Louis Prudent Vallée 1872
Collection: Public Archives of Canada, Ottawa,
PA 103073 (NPC-10)

26. The Breakneck Steps, Quebec City, Canada
East (Quebec)
Ellisson & Co. 1865
Collection: Public Archives of Canada, Ottawa,
PA 103125 (NPC-9)

27. Pointe Lévi, Quebec
Alexander Henderson c1870
Collection: Public Archives of Canada, Ottawa
(NPC-52)

28. "The Toboggan Party," Ottawa, Ontario
William James Topley c1875
Collection: Public Archives of Canada, Ottawa,
PA 8492 (NPC-5)

29. Ice cone, Montmorency Falls, Quebec
Alexander Henderson 1876
Collection: Public Archives of Canada, Ottawa
(NPC-59)

30. Skating in Victoria Rink, Montreal, Quebec
William Notman 1881
Collection: Notman Photographic Archives,
McCord Museum, Montreal

31. Mrs. Corriveau's baby
William Notman 1878
Collection: Notman Photographic Archives,
McCord Museum, Montreal

32. Tyne rowing crew, Lachine, Quebec
William Notman 1870
Collection: Notman Photographic Archives,
McCord Museum, Montreal

33. Women workers in the Huntington copper
mine, Bolton, Quebec
William Notman 1867
Collection: Notman Photographic Archives,
McCord Museum, Montreal

34. Mrs. William Mackenzie
William Notman 1871
Collection: Notman Photographic Archives,
McCord Museum, Montreal

35. Construction of the Intercolonial Railway,
Nova Scotia
1871
Collection: Public Archives of Canada, Ottawa,
PA 21998 (NPC-56)

36. Fort Chambly, Quebec
William Notman 1863
Collection: Notman Photographic Archives,
McCord Museum, Montreal

37. The Blanche River, Quebec
Alexander Henderson 1869
Collection: Notman Photographic Archives,
McCord Museum, Montreal

38. Murray Bay, Quebec
Alexander Henderson c1868
Collection: Ontario Archives, Toronto

39. Hunting scenes from Captain Grant's album
William Notman c1866
Collection: Public Archives of Canada, Ottawa
(NPC-54)

40. "A Thirsty Moose"
William Notman 1866
Collection: Public Archives of Canada, Ottawa
(NPC-53)

41. The prairie on the banks of Red River
Humphrey Lloyd Hime 1858
Collection: Manitoba Archives, Winnipeg, Hime
Collection 22

42. Bodies of Crow Indians, Sweetgrass Hills,
Royal Engineers 1873
Collection: Manitoba Archives, Winnipeg,
Boundary Commission (1872-74)181

43. German dancing girls at the Cariboo
goldfields, British Columbia
Frederick Dally c1868
Collection: Provincial Archives of British
Columbia, Victoria, 95344

44. Indian suspension bridge, British Columbia
Charles George Horetzky 1872
Collection: Public Archives of Canada, Ottawa,
PA 9133 (NPC-30)

45. Hunting still life, Vancouver Island, British
Columbia 1873-1877
Collection: Provincial Archives of British
Columbia, Victoria, 96190

46. Grave of a Couteaux chief, Lytton, British
Columbia
Frederick Dally 1867
Collection: Metropolitan Toronto Library

47. The Guy Tuttle residence, Yale, British
Columbia
Frederick Dally c1870
Collection: Provincial Archives of British
Columbia, Victoria, 9760

48. Studio fantasy, Victoria, British Columbia
Hannah Maynard c1893
Collection: Provincial Archives of British
Columbia, Victoria, 93164

49. Yan, Queen Charlotte Islands, British
Columbia
Edward Dossetter 1881
Collection: Provincial Archives of British
Columbia, Victoria, 33613

50. Loading lumber ships at Moodyville,
British Columbia
Richard Maynard c1887
Collection: Provincial Archives of British
Columbia, Victoria, 9305

51. Freight wagons and machinery at Yale,
British Columbia
Richard Maynard c1868
Collection: Provincial Archives of British
Columbia, Victoria, 9774

52. North West Mounted Police at Fort Macleod,
North West Territories (Alberta)
c1879
Collection: RCMP Museum, Regina

53. William Losee and family, Shawnigan Lake,
British Columbia
Jones and Company c1890
Collection: Provincial Archives of British
Columbia, 33945

54. Lumber shipment, Vancouver, British
Columbia
Baily Brothers c1890
Collection: Canadian Pacific Corporate Archives,
Montreal

55. Native longshoremen and Chinese laundrymen at Moodyville, British Columbia
c1889
Collection: City of Vancouver Archives,
Mi.P.2N.26

56. Haida Indians, Queen Charlotte Islands,
British Columbia
Edward Dossetter 1881
Collection: Provincial Archives of British
Columbia, Victoria, 33609

57. Pioneer bachelor's hall, Vancouver, British
Columbia
Baily Brothers 1890
Collection: City of Vancouver Archives, Bu.P131

58. Ottertail Bridge, CPR line, British Columbia
Richard H. Trueman c1897
Collection: Vancouver Public Library

59. View from Idaho Mines, British Columbia
Richard H. Trueman c1895
Collection: City of Vancouver Archives, CVA 2-34

60. Payne Bluff, Sandon, British Columbia
Richard H. Trueman 1900
Collection: City of Vancouver Archives, CVA 2-99

61. Blood Indian Sundance
William Hanson Boorne 1887
Collection: Notman Photographic Archives,
McCord Museum, Montreal

62. "Otokuyicokoan, Sarcee Indian"
William Hanson Boorne 1887
Collection: Notman Photographic Archives,
McCord Museum, Montreal

63. After the Northwest Rebellion
O.B. Buell 1885
Collection: Saskatchewan Archives Board, Regina,
R-B 741

64. Bull Head, Sarcee Chief
Alex J. Ross 1887
Collection: Notman Photographic Archives,
McCord Museum, Montreal

65. Graveyard at Fort Qu'Appelle, North West
Territories (Saskatchewan)
O.B. Buell 1885
Collection: Public Archives of Canada, Ottawa,
PA 118766 (NPC-58)

66. The Leader, Regina, North West Territories
(Saskatchewan)
O.B. Buell c1885
Collection: Public Archives of Canada, Ottawa,
PA 118776 (NPC-51)

67. Shackleton Brothers threshing outfit, North West Territories (Alberta)
C.W. Mathers c1898
Collection: Glenbow-Alberta Institute, Calgary, PA 58-104d

68. Round-up near Kamloops, British Columbia
Stephen J. Thompson c1895
Collection: The Whyte Museum, Banff

69. Portage, Slave River
C.W. Mathers 1901
Collection: Public Archives of Canada, Ottawa, (NPC-25)

70. Last Chance Hotel, Yukon Territory
c1900
Collection: Public Archives of Canada, Ottawa, C-59886 (NPC-26)

71. The Aurora Borealis over Dawson, Yukon Territory
Jerry Doody 1908
Collection: RCMP Museum, Regina

72. Palace Grand Theatre, Dawson, Yukon Territory
c1900
Collection: City of Vancouver Archives, P.1108 N651

73. Klondike Kate
1900
Collection: City of Vancouver Archives, Port P.990 N454

74. James Croil and Party
William Notman & Son 1888
Collection: Notman Photographic Archives, McCord Museum, Montreal

75. Montreal harbour, Quebec
William Notman c1875
Collection: Notman Photographic Archives, McCord Museum, Montreal

76. St. Catherine Street, Montreal, Quebec
William Notman & Son 1901
Collection: Notman Photographic Archives, McCord Museum, Montreal

77. Skiing at Rockcliffe Park, Ottawa, Ontario
William James Topley 1895
Collection: Public Archives of Canada, Ottawa, C43152 (NPC-27)

78. Flood in Montreal, Quebec
George Charles Arless 1886
Collection: Notman Photographic Archives, McCord Museum, Montreal

79. Charles Gurd's summer house near Montreal, Quebec
William Notman & Son c1886
Collection: Notman Photographic Archives, McCord Museum, Montreal

80. Pauline Johnson
Cochran c1895
Collection: Public Archives of Canada, Ottawa, C-85125 (NPC-49)

81. Parliament Buildings, Ottawa, Ontario
William Notman 1875
Collection: Notman Photographic Archives, McCord Museum, Montreal

82. Lady Marjorie Gordon
William James Topley 1898
Collection: Saskatchewan Archives Board, Regina, R-B 1146

83. Perley & Pattee sawmill, Ottawa, Ontario
William Notman 1872
Collection: Notman Photographic Archives, McCord Museum, Montreal

84. Steam drilling, Silver Lake Mine, Ontario
H.N. Topley c1908
Collection: Public Archives of Canada, Ottawa, (NPC-15)

85. Portsmouth Penitentiary, Kingston, Ontario
c1890
Collection: Queen's University Archives, Kingston

86. Bay Street following the fire of April 19, 1904, Toronto, Ontario
Henry F. Sharpe
Collection: Metropolitan Toronto Library

87. Toronto Island ferry terminal
Benjamin West Kilburn 1894
Collection: Ontario Archives, Toronto

88. The Knapp Roller Boat on Lake Ontario
William Thompson Freeland 1897
Collection: Public Archives of Canada, Ottawa, C-14063 (NPC-37)

89. Tourists at Niagara Falls
c1890
Collection: Canadian Pacific Corporate Archives, Montreal

90. Clifford M. Calverley on the wire over Whirlpool Rapids, Niagara River
Underwood & Underwood c1895
Collection: Ontario Archives, Toronto

91. Diorama painting, Victoria Memorial Museum, Ottawa, Ontario
1913
Collection: Public Archives of Canada, Ottawa, C-65508 (NPC-21)

92. Rocher Percé, Gaspé, Quebec
William Notman & Son c1905
Collection: Notman Photographic Archives, McCord Museum, Montreal

93. Murray Bay, Quebec
William Notman & Son 1900
Collection: Notman Photographic Archives, McCord Museum, Montreal

94. Rustico Beach, Prince Edward Island
William Notman & Son c1916
Collection: Notman Photographic Archives, McCord Museum, Montreal

95. Clearing a log jam, Ontario
c1890
Collection: Ontario Archives, Toronto.

96. Log jam, Grand Falls, New Brunswick
c1890
Collection: The New Brunswick Museum, Saint John (0016A 1-6)

97. Bridges over the Reversing Falls, Saint John, New Brunswick
William Notman & Son c1898
Collection: Notman Photographic Archives, McCord Museum, Montreal

98. Workmen with carved salmon, Saint John, New Brunswick
Isaac Erb c1910
Collection: Wilson Studio, Saint John

99. Laying a macadam road, Saint John, New Brunswick
Isaac Erb c1900
Courtesy: Wilson Studio, Saint John

100. Odevaine family and friends at York Redoubt, Nova Scotia
1898
Collection: Public Archives of Nova Scotia, Halifax

101. Halifax fireman
Parish & Co. c1870
Collection: Nova Scotia Museum, Halifax, P29 65.115

102. Hopewell Cape, Bay of Fundy, New Brunswick
William Notman & Son c1900
Courtesy: Notman Photographic Archives, McCord Museum, Montreal

103. Lily pond near Kentville, Nova Scotia
Amos Lawson Hardy c1896
Collection: Public Archives of Canada, Ottawa, PA 126488 (NPC-4)

104. Group and Stanley Steamer, Kentville, Nova Scotia
c1902
Collection: Nova Scotia Museum, Halifax, P135 73.99

105. Steel mill at North Sydney, Cape Breton Island, Nova Scotia
Isaac Erb c1904
Collection: Wilson Studio, Saint John

106. A victim of the fire, Windsor, Nova Scotia
1897
Collection: Public Archives of Nova Scotia, Halifax

107. Marconi's towers, Cape Breton Island, Nova Scotia
Isaac Erb c1904
Collection: Wilson Studio, Saint John

108. H.D. Reid's automobile at Signal Hill, St. John's, Newfoundland
William Notman & Son 1908
Collection: Notman Photographic Archives, McCord Museum, Montreal

109. "The guns used in firing the Royal Salute"
James Vey 1901
Collection: Provincial Archives of Newfoundland and Labrador, St. John's

110. Squid jigging in Burin, Newfoundland
Robert E. Holloway c1900
Collection: Provincial Archives of Newfoundland and Labrador, St. John's

111. Pouch Cove, Newfoundland
Robert E. Holloway 1900
Collection: Public Archives of Canada, Ottawa, PA 121936 (NPC-6)

112. Under the cod drying flakes, St. John's, Newfoundland
Simeon H. Parsons 1880
Collection: Centre for Newfoundland Studies, Memorial University, St. John's

113. Sealers copying the floes, Newfoundland
Robert E. Holloway c1920
Collection: Provincial Archives of Newfoundland and Labrador, St. John's

114. The *Arctic* at Port Burwell, Ungava (Quebec)
George R. Lancefield 1907
Collection: Public Archives of Canada, Ottawa, PA 96482 (NPC-34)

115. She-nuck-shoo, Eskimo chief
Geraldine Moodie 1905-06
Collection: British Museum, London, England

116. Koo-tuck-tuck, Eskimo girl
Geraldine Moodie 1905-06
Collection: British Museum, London, England

117. Kayak in floes
Robert Flaherty 1920-21
Collection: Notman Photographic Archives, McCord Museum, Montreal

118. HMS *Discovery* in winter quarters, Ellesmere Island
Thomas Mitchell 1875-76
Collection: Public Archives of Canada, Ottawa, C-52573 (NPC-23)

119. Topek, Kayak and Eskimo, Peel River, North West Territories
C.W. Mathers 1901
Collection: Public Archives of Canada, Ottawa, (NPC-2)

120. Elliott Barnes in his cabin at Kootenay Plains, Alberta
Elliott Barnes 1907
Collection: The Whyte Museum, Banff

121. Western Anemone
Mary M. Vaux c1910
Collection: The Whyte Museum, Banff

122. Sampson Beaver and family
Mary T.S. Schäffer 1906
Collection: The Whyte Museum, Banff

123. Lois and Oscar Barnes at Sawback Lake, Canadian Rockies
Elliott Barnes 1906-08
Collection: The Whyte Museum, Banff

124. Mount Temple in cloud from Ptarmigan Valley, Canadian Rockies
Vaux family 1906
Collection: The Whyte Museum, Banff

125. Mount Resplendent, Canadian Rockies
Byron Harmon 1913
Collection: The Whyte Museum, Banff

126. Bow Lake, Canadian Rockies
Byron Harmon 1924
Collection: the author.

127. T.H. Beach, rancher, near Gleichen, Alberta
c1910
Collection: Glenbow-Alberta Institute, Calgary, PA 505-3

128. Oil boom in Calgary, Alberta
Harry Pollard 1914
Collection: Provincial Archives of Alberta, Edmonton, P1135

129. J.W. Millar's hemp crop, North Battleford, Saskatchewan
Harry Pollard 1920
Collection: Provincial Archives of Alberta, Edmonton, P665

130. Model T Ford at Eastburg, Alberta
c1920
Collection: Provincial Archives of Alberta, Edmonton, A8996

131. Lillie Reeves with marrows, Edmonton, Alberta
Ernest Brown 1907
Collection: Provincial Archives of Alberta, Edmonton, B 6818

132. Apples, Kentville, Nova Scotia
Amos Lawson Hardy 1911
Collection: Public Archives of Canada, Ottawa, PA 135455 (NPC-41)

133. Vegetables from D. Ross's garden, Edmonton, North West Territories (Alberta)
C.W. Mathers 1902
Collection: Notman Photographic Archives, McCord Museum, Montreal

134. Advertisement for McClary stoves
1897
Collection: Public Archives of Canada, Ottawa, PA 28854 (NPC-42)

135. "The Way We Harvest Wheat"
Canadian Postcard Company c1912
Collection: Public Archives of Canada, Ottawa, C-8708 (NPC-38)

136. Mounted wolf heads
William Hanson Boorne c1893
Collection: Glenbow-Alberta Institute, Calgary,
PA 1001-41

137. Hunting party, Lake of the Woods, Ontario
C.G. Linde 1913
Collection: Public Archives of Canada, Ottawa,
PA 30070 (NPC-43)

138. Bear wrestling
c1902
Collection: Public Archives of Canada, Ottawa,
C-14070 (NPC-36)

139. Men with crocuses, Lumsden, Saskatchewan
William M. Tegart 1910
Collection: Saskatchewan Archives Board, Regina,
R-B 163

140. Granby Mine, Phoenix, British Columbia
c1905
Collection: Provincial Archives of British
Columbia, Victoria, 18379

141. Reserve Mine, Nanaimo, British Columbia
c1920
Collection: Provincial Archives of British
Columbia, Victoria, 18723

142. Salmon fishing, British Columbia
Edwards Brothers 1903
Collection: City of Vancouver Archives, CVA
102.25

143. Unidentified portrait, Vancouver Island,
British Columbia
c1905
Collection: Public Archives of Canada, Ottawa
(NPC-46)

144. Stanley Park, Vancouver, British Columbia
c1908
Collection: Provincial Archives of British
Columbia, Victoria, 33108

145. "A Girl From Canada"
T.A. Chandler 1907
Collection: Public Archives of Canada, Ottawa,
C-63256 (NPC-7)

146. Celebration, southern Ontario
William James c1906
Collection: City of Toronto Archives, James 1900

147. Mr. and Mrs. George H. Hees
William James c1911
Collection: City of Toronto Archives, James 1824

148. Motorcade for Sir Wilfrid Laurier
1911
Collection: Public Archives of Canada, Ottawa,
C-24798 (NPC-31)

149. Hitch-hikers in Muddy York (Toronto),
Ontario
William James c1907
Collection: City of Toronto Archives, James 36

150. Workers with steam hammer
William James c1910
Collection: City of Toronto Archives, James 114

151. Carving an Ionic capital, Winnipeg,
Manitoba
Foote & James 1915
Collection: Manitoba Archives, Winnipeg, Foote
587 (N2187)

152. The CPR's Lethbridge Viaduct across the
Oldman River, Alberta
1909
Collection: The Whyte Museum, Banff

153. Remains of the first Quebec Bridge
1907
Collection: Public Archives of Canada, Ottawa,
PA 109498 (NPC-48)
Dominion Bridge Company Collection

154. Workmen with a link for the second Quebec
Bridge
Eugene Michael Finn 1915
Collection: Public Archives of Canada, Ottawa
(NPC-12)

155. Waterfront at the Canadian National
Exhibition grounds, Toronto, Ontario
William James c1909
Collection: City of Toronto Archives, James 1803

156. After the fire at the Kelly Block, Winnipeg,
Manitoba
Lewis B. Foote 1911
Collection: Manitoba Archives, Winnipeg,
Foote 228 (N1828)

157. The fresh-air cure for tuberculosis, Toronto,
Ontario
Arthur Goss 1912
Collection: City of Toronto Archives,
Health 31-154

158. A ward of the Children's Aid Society,
Stratford, Ontario
Young Shannon c1895
Collection: Public Archives of Canada, Ottawa,
PA 123673 (NPC-8)

159. Children in "The Ward," Toronto, Ontario
William James c1908
Collection: City of Toronto Archives, James 659

160. Girl with raven
Reuben R. Sallows c1910
Collection: Public Archives of Canada, Ottawa
(NPC-3)

161. Child's funeral, Toronto, Ontario
William James c1910
Collection: City of Toronto Archives, James 37/41

162. Senior baseball, Toronto, Ontario
1915
Collection: City of Toronto Archives,
Parks 52-515

163. Roy Campbell vs Dick Hyland, Vancouver,
British Columbia
W.J. Cairns 1913
Collection: City of Vancouver Archives, Sp. P. 98

164. The first all-Canadian aircraft, Baddeck
No. 1
1909
Collection: Public Archives of Canada, Ottawa,
C-20260 (NPC-11)

165. A performer at the Canadian National
Exhibition, Toronto, Ontario
William James c1912
Collection: City of Toronto Archives, James 2174

166. Dr. Margaret Patterson and cow, Toronto,
Ontario
c1914
Collection: Ontario Archives, Toronto, RG 10

167. Diving horse, Hanlan's Point, Toronto,
Ontario
William James c1908
Collection: City of Toronto Archives, James 191

168. Bridal party, Toronto, Ontario
William James c1910
Collection: City of Toronto Archives, James 7/37

169. Miss Billings and friends
William Notman & Son 1915
Collection: Notman Photographic Archives,
McCord Museum, Montreal

170. Off to War, Toronto, Ontario
William James 1916
Collection: City of Toronto Archives, James 829

171. Military guard on the Quebec Bridge
Eugene Michael Finn 1916
Collection: Public Archives of Canada, Ottawa
(NPC-14)

172. War production, Woodstock, Ontario
1918
Collection: Public Archives of Canada, Ottawa,
PA 24499 (NPC-24)

173. Campbell Road following the explosion,
Halifax, Nova Scotia
1917
Collection: Nova Scotia Museum, Halifax, P17
76.91.83

174. Trench warfare demonstration, Toronto,
Ontario
William James c1914
Collection: City of Toronto Archives, James 966

175. Tank demonstration, Toronto, Ontario
William James 1918
Collection: City of Toronto Archives, James 733

176. Canadian troops in France
1914-1918
Collection: City of Vancouver Archives,
Gr.War. P.18

177. Troopship *Olympic* in dazzle paint, Halifax,
Nova Scotia
British and Colonial Press 1919
Collection: Public Archives of Canada, Ottawa
PA 30304 (NPC-39)

178. Returning troops, Halifax, Nova Scotia
British and Colonial Press 1919
Collection: Public Archives of Canada, Ottawa,
PA 22995 (NPC-47)

179. Riding demonstration, Toronto, Ontario
William James c1920
Collection: City of Toronto Archives, James 23/2

180. During the Winnipeg General Strike,
Manitoba
British and Colonial Press 1919
Collection: RCMP Museum, Regina

181. Ku Klux Klan members, Vancouver,
British Columbia
Stuart Thomson 1925
Collection: City of Vancouver Archives,
CVA99-1496

182. Speed skaters
William James 1924
Collection: City of Toronto Archives, James 37/36

183. Crowd watching a Human Fly,
Toronto, Ontario
William James c1920
Collection: City of Toronto Archives, James 949

184. Demonstrating a radiophone
Frederick McDermid 1922
Collection: Glenbow-Alberta Institute, Calgary,
NC6-10155

185. Ferris wheels, Canadian National
Exhibition, Toronto, Ontario
William James 1924
Collection: City of Toronto Archives, James 2017

186. Foul Bay beach and Gonzales Heights,
Victoria, British Columbia
Gus A. Maves c1920
Collection: Provincial Archives of British
Columbia, Victoria, 96192

187. Marathon swim preparations,
Toronto, Ontario
William James c1927
Collection: City of Toronto Archives, James 18/2

188. Prince of Wales and Prince George,
Winnipeg, Manitoba
Lewis B. Foote 1927
Collection: Manitoba Archives, Winnipeg,
Foote 336 (N1936)

189. Poultry class at Olds College, Olds, Alberta
Frederick McDermid 1921
Collection: Glengow-Alberta Institute, Calgary,
ND-932

190. Strawberry pickers, Vancouver Island,
British Columbia
Gus A. Maves c1920
Collection: Provincial Archives of British
Columbia, Victoria, 96191

191. Theatre lantern slide
1912
Collection: The Whyte Museum, Banff

Selected Bibliography

For an overview of Canadian history:
Brebner, John Bartlet. *The North Atlantic Triangle: The Interplay of Canada, The United States and Great Britain.* New Haven: Yale University Press, 1945.

Callwood, June. *Portrait of Canada.* Toronto: Doubleday, 1981.

Creighton, Donald. *Canada's First Century 1867 – 1967.* Toronto: Macmillan, 1970.

Lower, Arthur R.M. *Colony to Nation: A History of Canada.* 5th Ed. Toronto: McClelland & Stewart, 1977.

Morton, Desmond. *A Short History of Canada.* Edmonton: Hurtig, 1983.

Morton, W.L. ed. *The Shield of Achilles: Aspects of Canada in the Victorian Age.* Toronto/Montreal: McClelland & Stewart, 1968.

Stacey, C.P. *Canada and the Age of Conflict: A History of Canadian External Policies.* Macmillan, 1977.

For the joy of reading history first hand:
Butler, Sir William Francis. *The Great Lone Land: A Tale of Travel and Adventure in the North West of America.* London: Sampson Low, Marston, Low & Searle, 1872.

Dufferin and Ava, Marchioness of. *My Canadian Journal.* London: John Murray, 1891.

Grant, the Reverend George M. *Ocean to Ocean: Sandford Fleming's Expedition through Canada in 1872.* Toronto: James Campbell & Son, 1873.

Milton, Viscount and W. B. Cheadle. *The North West Passage by Land: Being the Narrative of an Expedition from the Atlantic to the Pacific....* London: Cassel, Petter and Galpin, 1865.

Photography
Bernard, Bruce. *Photodiscovery: Masterworks of Photography 1840 – 1940.* New York: Harry N. Abrams, 1980.

Crawford, William. *The Keepers of Light: A History and Working Guide to Early Photographic Processes.* New York: Morgan and Morgan, 1979.

Daval, Jean-Luc. *Photography: History of an Art.* New York: Skira/Rizzoli, 1982.

Gernsheim, Helmut and Alison. *The History of Photography from the Camera Obscura to the Beginning of the Modern Era.* New York: McGraw-Hill, 1969.

Greenhill, Ralph, and Andrew Birrell. *Canadian Photography: 1839 – 1920.* Toronto: The Coach House Press, 1979.

Harper, J. Russell, and Stanley Triggs eds. *Portrait of a Period: A Collection of Notman Photographs 1856 to 1915.* Montreal: McGill University Press, 1967.

Newhall, Beaumont. *The History of Photography from 1839 to the Present.* 2nd Ed. New York: The Museum of Modern Art, 1982.

About the Author

Edward Cavell was born in 1948 at Lachine, Quebec, and was educated in Montreal, at Stanstead College in the Eastern Townships of Quebec, and at Mount Allison University in Sackville, New Brunswick. In 1968 he moved to Banff, where he found his vocation in the photography programme of the Banff Centre. His research on the history of photography in western Canada provided the basis for his first book, *Journeys to the Far West*, published in 1979 by James Lorimer and Company. Three other books followed: *A Delicate Wilderness: The Photography of Elliott Barnes*, 1981; *Rocky Mountain Madness, A Bittersweet Romance*, co-authored with Jon Whyte, 1982; and *Legacy in Ice: The Vaux Family and the Canadian Alps*, 1983.

For *Sometimes a Great Nation*, Cavell embarked on a search of the vast photographic holdings in the major archives across Canada. By his own description, the author's journey of discovery is a love affair with his own country, Canada.

"My fascination about who we are and why grew to a passion as I was seduced by photograph upon photograph. I was wooed by images of beautiful women and brokenhearted by the thought of their passing. I suffered vertigo, induced by a top-hatted man who sat on the edge of Rideau Falls well over a hundred years ago. I discovered how cobblestones were laid, sewers were built, how fish were caught and timber was shipped. I was overwhelmed by the Gothic grandeur of the first Parliament Buildings and intrigued by the faces of the thousands of nameless people who had gone before. Images of love, death, prejudice, war, solitude and happiness swirled by in a never-ending stream. I became a time traveller, a cultural voyeur, privy to the public and private lives that constitute the history of Canada."

Edward Cavell lives in Banff and is Curator of Photography at the Whyte Museum of the Canadian Rockies.

Acknowledgements

The photographs in this book have been selected from the millions of images held in twenty-four collections spread across Canada from St. John's, Newfoundland, to Victoria, British Columbia. The photographs, with the exception of those from one corporate, one foreign and two private collections, are all public property, a vast visual heritage held in trust for the people of Canada by several levels of government and institutions. Without the generous support and co-operation of these agencies and the people who manage them, this publication would not have been possible.

The quality and the accessibility of a collection are ultimately the responsibility of the people who care for it; the photographs in this book stand as testament to the dedication and skill of the archivists and curators who are the keepers of our past. A number of these individuals have aided greatly in the research for this book; out of respect, admiration and appreciation I mention the following: Andrew Birrell, Elizabeth Blight, Margaret Campbell, John Crosthwait, J. Robert Davidson, Jean Dryden, Jean Goldie, Nancy Gren-

ville, Cecil Halsey, Joy Houston, Jonathan King, Georgeen Klassen, Lilly Koltun, Omer Lavallée, Ken Macpherson, Ed McCann, Leslie Mobbs, Jerry Mossop, Anthony Murphy, Peter Robinson, Scott Robson, Leslie Ross, Karen Teeple, Ann Thomas, James Wilson and Ken Young. The collections from which the photographs have been drawn are all credited in the list of plates.

I would like to thank in particular two people who freely shared their time and knowledge: Joan Schwartz of the National Photography Collection and Stanley Triggs of the Notman Photographic Archives. The time spent poring over photographs with them was truly a joy.

Shirley Barwise of the Department of the Secretary of State and Bess Clare of the Historic Yale Museum at Yale, B.C., are thanked for their assistance in the pursuit of information.

A selected bibliography is included separately. I would, however, like to mention three historians whose works have introduced me to, and revealed the delights of, the complexities of Canadian history: Donald Creighton, Arthur R.M. Lower and W.L. Morton.

My understanding of the history of photography is largely based on the work of Helmut and Alison Gernsheim and Beaumont Newhall. The specifics of Canadian photography I credit to Ralph Greenhill and Andrew Birrell. Bruce Bernard's stunning book *Photodiscovery* has been an important influence and inspiration in the formation of the concept for this endeavour.

The editors of this publication served far beyond the call of duty. My thanks to Jane and Martin Lynch for the world of information they have added. This book is as much a reflection of their appreciation of fact as my fascination for photography.

My friends and my cohorts at the Whyte Museum in Banff are to be thanked for their understanding and forbearance as I was totally distracted and consumed by this project. A special appreciation goes to Erin Michie for her help in preparing the manuscript.

Beyond anything that I have done, this book is the product of the unbounded faith, committment and vision of the publishers – Carole Harmon and Stephen Hutchings.

Thank you all.
Edward Cavell, June, 1984.

Design: Scott Thornley, TDA
Art Production: Mark Glowienko, Bruce Aitken, TDA
Production Assistance: Margaret Deveaux, TDA
Typesetting: Crocker Bryant Inc.

Editing: Jane and Martin Lynch
Proofreading: Barbara MacLennan

Colour Separations and Printing: Dai Nippon
Printed and bound in Japan